The Crafty D
Lifestyle Makeover

AWESOME Ideas to SPICE Up Your LIFE!

by
Kathy Cano
Murillo

Illustrated by
Carrie Wheeler

Photography by
John Samora

Watson-Guptill Publications/New York

Senior Acquisitions Editor: Julie Mazur
Designer: Margo Mooney
Senior Production Manager: Ellen Greene
Text set in 9.5 pt. Gotham Book

First published in 2005 by
Watson-Guptill Publications,
a division of VNU Business Media, Inc.
770 Broadway, New York, NY 10003
www.wgpub.com

Library of Congress Cataloging-in-Publication Data

Cano-Murillo, Kathy.
        The crafty diva's lifestyle makeover : awesome ideas to spice up your
life / by Kathy Cano Murillo ; illustrated by Carrie Wheeler ; photography by John Samora.
            p. cm.
        ISBN 0-8230-1008-2
1. Handicraft for girls—Juvenile literature. I. Title.
        TT171.C36 2005
        745.5—dc22
                        2004024342

Printed in China.

First printing, 2005

1 2 3 4 5 6 7 8 / 12 11 10 09 08 07 06 05

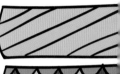

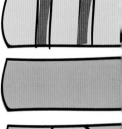
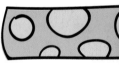

This book is dedicated to my mom, Norma Jean, who inspired my craftiness at an early age. From her handmade Halloween costumes to balloon wall decorations made of felt, I learned from the best!

Contents

Introduction: Are You Ready for a Makeover?

The answer is "yes" if...

❀ Your hair automatically falls into the same shape every day.

❀ The contents of your closet are as exciting as homework on a Friday night.

❀ Your friends can predict what you'll eat for lunch.

❀ The cute guy sitting next to you in math still calls you "Hey you!"

Okay, stop—this is getting depressing! If you said "um *hmm*!" to at least one of the above, it's time to stop and check yourself. No, check your *life*! Yes, you are absolutely adorable the way you are, but a little makeover magic always helps spice things up. Especially on those days when you have the frump-girl blues or are just plain bored with your daily routine. *The Crafty Diva's Lifestyle Makeover* is your one-stop shop to get things rolling. It won't be long before you are cutting, pasting, gluing, and sprinkling your way to a new and adventurous way of looking and thinking!

Flip through these pages to find an over-flowing gift basket of crafty ideas, all designed to add more pop to your popularity, flava to your food, and sass to your style. Tired of tossing out old clothes and toys you've outgrown? We'll show you how to get more mileage out of them. Sick of feeling shy and unsure of yourself? We'll show you how to break out of your shell. Want to make money but don't like lemonade? We'll teach you how to set up a rad yard sale! Follow the tips in each chapter and you'll go from shy girl to fly girl in no time at all.

So what exactly does "makeover" mean?

No matter what our age, we all fall into ruts now and then. You know the feeling. You look in the mirror and say, "Holy cupcakes, I need a change!" Maybe it's when the stuffed bunnies on your Pretty Princess comforter suddenly seem more corny than cute. Or when your jewelry box won't close because it's too full of plastic earrings from several birthday parties ago. And your clothing options? We won't even go there.... Sometimes you can just wave your magic crafty wand (with the help of glue and scissors) and bring the spring back into lackluster items. And then there are things that (*sniff!*) are just meant to be sold at the next family yard sale.

You'll find that revamping everything in sight is cooler than ice cream in an igloo. But hold up, little missy. This makeover isn't just about making stuff look good, it's also about working on your mind, body, and soul. Taking time to shake up your style, tastes, thoughts, and attitudes will keep you growing, learning, and feeling good. And if you feel good on the inside, it will shine through to the outside!

Ready, set, go! *Almost*....

Making over your life is no easy trick. To help you get started, warm up your creative juices by taking the Spice Up Your Life quiz on page 7. That way you'll know which chapters to try first. Oh, and check out the Crafty Rundown chapter that covers all the supplies you'll need. Last but not least, don't miss the treasure trove of clip art in the back of the book (pages 140–141) that you can use in your projects.

SPICE UP YOUR LIFE!

There are so many dilemmas to ponder. How can we get world peace? How can I ever afford an iPod? What part of my life should I make over first? I don't know about the first two, but the last one is as easy as walking through the front door of The Sims. Here's the dealio, chica. Answer the questions below, then total your score to find out which part of your life needs 911 attention first. Got it? Have fun!

QUIZ

1. What is your worst fear when it comes to your room?

  A. Having to sort through all those outdated clothes stuffed in the bottom drawer of your dresser.

  B. Changing anything, even if it's just scooting a picture frame over one millimeter.

  C. Getting totally into a book or art project and being interrupted by a parent or sibling.

2. Someday you secretly hope to featured on:

  A. *America's Next Top Model,* so you can finally get discovered.

  B. *Ambush Makeover,* because deep down you yearn for a makeover but are too chicken to admit it.

  C. *Ripley's Believe It or Not,* for your amazing collection of Orlando Bloom posters.

3. You get to help plan your best friend's birthday bash. You choose to be in charge of:

  A. The whole thing. No one else could do it better!

  B. Nothing. Let everyone else do the work!

  C. Crafty things, like making the posters, invites, and thank-you cards.

4. If you could get exercise any way you wanted, it would be:

  A. Four hours of nonstop *Dance Dance Revolution* at a Friday night party.

  B. Just as you do it now. Why fix something that ain't broken?

  C. Working up a sweat making funky posters about the upcoming Earth Day festival.

5. You have $100. What do you spend it on?

  A. A funky purse, a silky eye mask, yummy-smelling bubble bath, and a subscription to your favorite magazine.

  B. Newer versions of clothes you already own but have outgrown.

  C. A huge set of multicolor double-sided markers, scrapbook supplies, a pad of pretty recycled paper, and a cool-looking wind chime.

SCORING: Give yourself 3 points for each "a" answer, 1 point for each "b" answer, and 2 points for each "c" answer.

5–7 points: Girl, you need to break out of your humdrum routine. Say buh-bye to old habits—it's time to liven things up! Check out these chapters: Redo Your Room, Dare to Be Social, Find Your Flava, Love Your Locker, Make Some Money, and Jazz Your Jewelry.

8–12 points: You have gobs of friends, but you're just as happy spending time at home with fresh paintbrushes and a journal. That's all well and good, but somewhere deep inside is a drama fashionista yearning to come out. Don't hold her back! Take a look-see at these chapters: Pamper Your Inner Princess, Amp Up Your Accessories, Wake Up Your Workout, Get a Passion for Fashion, Gift with Glam, and Tune In.

13–15 points: You are loud and proud! You crave attention, yearn for drama, and love to work up a sweat. But how about tapping into your quiet side for a change? Try these chapters to help your makeover be a strong and silent one: Take an Artsy Adventure, Free Your Words, Become a Nature Nut, Soothe Your Spirit, and Save the Earth.

The Crafty Rundown

Want everything you make to come out chic enough for a fashion runway show? That won't happen unless you use the right supplies. Some things you can find around the house, others you'll have to tip your piggy bank for. Don't forget to check newspaper ads for coupons and sales!

TIP

When you work with paint, keep a plastic tray for mixing, a cup of water, and paper towels nearby. To clean a brush between colors, swirl it in the water, then carefully dry it on a paper towel. Oh, and always rinse your brush before setting it down—it will last much longer!

Paints

Here are the brands of paint I use. They've been tried and tested with amazing results!

Craft acrylic paint: These water-based, nontoxic paints come in 2-ounce bottles. I like Delta Ceramcoat acrylics, which provide excellent coverage. They work on any kind of surface—fabric, plastic, wood, metal, even rocks—and will stay put as long as you apply varnish over them. Make a list of your favorite colors so you'll remember them when you get to the store. (Dry time: 15–20 minutes)

3-D squeeze paint: This paint is smooth and thick, like icing. It comes in a tiny bottle with a small hole for writing. My favorite brand is Scribbles. (Dry time: At least 1 hour)

Enamel paint: This kind of paint works on dishes and mugs. But only use it on the areas that *don't* touch food. I like Delta Air-Dry PermEnamel. (Dry time: 1 hour)

Paintbrushes

You'll need wide foam or soft-bristle brushes for base-coating and varnishing large surfaces. You'll also want thin liner brushes for outlining and adding details.

Pens

There are more kinds of pens than there are candy flavors! You don't *need* all of these, but they sure are nifty to have around.

Paint pen: A black, silver, or gold paint pen is great for outlining or adding accents. Don't forget to shake it before you use it.

Metallic markers: I like Sharpie markers best. They work well on paper crafts such as journals, cards, and scrapbooks—and for giving autographs, too.

Fabric pens: Don't feel like using wet paint? I don't blame you. Forget the mess and try these little babies instead. The ink dries soft and bendable so the fabric won't get stiff.

Colored markers: A girl can never have too many markers. Look for ones that have two different tips (one thin and one thick). If you have extra money, go for the glittered kind.

Glitter

Glitter for world peace, that's what I always say. A dash of glitz will make your project go from flat to fabulous in no time. The best way to use loose or micro-glitter is to lay a piece of paper on the table first. Sprinkle the glitter onto your project, then tap off the extra—the paper will keep it from going all over the place. Then you can carefully pick up the paper, bend it in half, and pour the extra glitter back into the container.

Squeeze-on glitter paint: This is just like the 3-D Scribbles paint mentioned above, except it sparkles.

Polyester microfine glitter: Think fairy dust. It's ultrafine and oh-so-pretty.

Fabric glitter spray: I like Tulip Permanent Fabric Glitter Spray. It comes in a small plastic spray bottle and can be used on most fabrics (but not hair or skin!). (Dry time: 15–20 minutes)

Loose glitter: This is the thick, grainy stuff we've come to know and love.

Glues and Adhesives

Glue is a must-have for crafting. Read on to see the different kinds and when to use them.

White glue: Everyone has a bottle of Elmer's glue lying around. It works perfectly for general crafting, and dries clear. If you already have this at home, go for it. (Dry time: 15 minutes, longer for thicker layers)

Crafter's Pick "The Ultimate" craft glue: This adhesive is my new best friend. It bonds just about anything, from metal to paper to fabric. It is water-based, dries clear, and holds tighter than a lid on a new jar of pickles. I put it on everything except my cereal in the morning. Just kidding. (Dry time: 20 minutes, longer for thicker layers; a full 24 hours to "cure")

Fabric glue: If you've never used a sewing machine, use this glue instead to add trims or fabric shapes to clothing. The best brand is Aleene's OK To Wash-It—like the name says, it's okay to wash it! (Dry time: 20 minutes)

E6000 Industrial Strength Adhesive: Use this glue when you need a heavy-duty hold. It is gooey, clear, and dries thick and rubbery. (Dry time: 10 minutes to "set"; a full 24 hours to "cure")

Glue sticks: Any brand will do—just buy a package of four, because you'll go through them pretty fast. (Dry time: 10 minutes)

Double-sided tape: For use with lightweight paper or fabric projects (in place of straight pins). I like Terrifically Tacky Tape, found in craft stores.

Mod Podge: This is a creamy, white, glue-like mixture that is used for decoupage, which is the art of covering a surface with paper. You simply brush it on any surface, place your paper on top, and then brush on another layer of Mod Podge. It seals the paper down nice and slick. If you don't have Mod Podge, white glue will work, too. (Dry time: 20 minutes)

Varnishes and Sealers

After all that work, you'll want to make sure your masterpieces last as long as Madonna's career. Here's how to seal the deal.

Water-based varnish: This varnish is super safe and can be used right in your bedroom. If you buy *gloss* varnish, it will give a high shine to your work. *Matte* varnish gives a dull glaze. Apply with a foam brush you use just for varnishing and rinse the brush after each use. (Dry time: 30 minutes)

Spray varnish: This varnish comes in a can, like spray paint. Any time you use it, make sure you are wearing a paper mask to keep from breathing in any fumes, and only use it outside. If you have to choose between brush-on varnish and spray varnish, go with the brush-on kind. (Dry time: 30 minutes)

Sparkle varnish: Delta Sparkle Varnish is a water-based, high-gloss liquid that will leave light flecks of pink and blue glitter on any type of surface. (Dry time: 20 minutes)

Scissors

Mini scissors are great for getting into teeny corners, and curvy or zigzag scissors make cool-shaped cuts. But a brand-new pair of the regular kind will be just fine.

Jewelry and Wire-working Tools

Whether you want to make accessories to wear or to sell, you really need the correct tools.

Jump rings: These are small silver or gold rings that connect one thing to another. Pick up a pack of rings that measure $\frac{1}{4}$ to $\frac{1}{2}$ inch in diameter (1 to 2 cm) and you're set.

Wire: Wire comes in all kinds of colors and widths. Standard wire is 24 gauge—the number tells you how thick or thin the wire is. The higher the number, the skinnier the wire. The lower the number, the thicker the wire.

Needle-nose pliers: Use these to twist and curl wire into any shape. You can also use them to cut wire, thanks to a tiny clipper at the bottom. If you don't have a pair and only plan on making one wire project, you can go

OUCH! Any time you use a spray product, you *must* wear a paper mask to keep from breathing in poison fumes. And only use such products outside, never in the house!

without, or use old tweezers instead. Keep in mind that cutting wire with regular scissors will damage them, so if you plan on going wire crazy, definitely pick up a set of these pliers.

Papers, Pictures, Rubber Stamps, and Stencils

It's not just about cutting up magazines anymore! Check the yellow pages to find scrapbooking stores in your neighborhood—they'll have all kinds of rubber stamps, stencils, pictures, and papers. Also look for things like wallpaper, postcards, old school books and encyclopedias, note cards, photos, stickers, and ticket stubs. Ask your parents if they have any old family photos you can use.

Fabric and Clothing

Your mom will be thrilled when she sees you cleaning out your closet—and then she'll freak when you tell her you are about to "alter" it all. Aways ask permission before cutting anything up. After you have the all-clear, gather items like shirts, pants, bags, scarves, hankies, socks,

shoelaces, and belts that are prime for a makeover. If you don't have anything that looks promising, visit secondhand shops to see if they have stuff you can pick up for cheap.

Found Objects

These are everyday objects that are normally found in the junk drawer or even the (gasp!) trash. Buttons, charms, coins, stamps, magnetic poetry pieces, earrings, small toys, game pieces, stickers—things like this add an electrifying edge to your masterpiece.

Sequins, Beads, Gems, and Rhinestones

Want to add a bit of glamour to your one-of-a-kind designs? I like to buy these in bulk because they are cheaper that way and you'll always have some on hand.

Sewing and Embroidery

If you are bold and brave enough to tackle sewing, you'll need a needle, thread, and straight pins. For embroidery, pick up a hoop, embroidery floss, and an embroidery needle.

HOW TO SEW BY HAND

Some projects ask you to sew with a needle and thread. Here's how to do a basic stitch.

1. Cut a piece of thread 24 inches long. Lick the end to make a sharp point. Hold your needle up to the light and insert the end of the thread through the hole.

2. Pull the thread until it's doubled, with the needle in the middle. Tie the ends together in a double knot.

3. Poke the needle through from the underside of the fabric. Gently pull the needle and thread until it stops.

4. Skip about ¼ inch of space and poke the needle back down through the fabric, again pulling until it stops.

5. Skip another ¼ inch of space. Poke the needle back up through the fabric and pull.

6. Keep going! If you're sewing a hem, work in a line along the edge of the fabric. When you reach the end, sew an extra stitch over your last one to secure. Flip over the fabric and make a double knot on the underside so your stitches stay put.

Makeover 101

To be cool on the outside, you have to feel cool on the inside. So to get this makeover started, take a minute to think about your life right now. What are the areas that could use some excitement? Make a list of the things you have always wanted to add sparkle to but never had the time or nerve. Tape the list on your wall or write it on the cover of your notebook. Use it as a reminder to take a chance every day. If, for example, one of your things is to be less shy, you can try to say hi to one new person each day. Get it?

Once you know what parts of your daily agenda need attention, then you can reach for the glue and scissors! But hold on, making stuff over isn't just about taking any old thing and slapping some glitter on it. As any designer will tell you, there's an art to it. The makeover gods have spoken. Please read this list of lessons learned.

❀ Create a special place in your room to get crafty. It can be a card table in the corner, a fold-up TV tray, or a nightstand.

❀ Keep all of your supplies sorted so you don't waste time looking for them. If you use boxes, label them.

❀ Don't just make over something for the sake of trying it. What good is a made-over chair if the chair is too rickety to sit on? You just wasted all those supplies—the horror! Take a minute to think about what will make the best re-dos before diving in.

❀ If you are taking on a big project, like totally revamping your room or closet, do it like *Trading Spaces* does. Start by coming up with a goal or theme, drawing some sketches, and making a list of things you need. Then remove everything in the area and get rid of any dust bunnies. Decide which things to part with (shoes you outgrew three years ago), which things are good makeover candi-

dates (last year's Halloween costume), and which things are fine to leave as they are (your brand-new winter coat).

❀ Read all instructions—twice—before starting.

❀ Arrange and rearrange items to make sure you like the design before gluing them down.

❀ Work on one project at a time and don't rush.

❀ Sign all of your work or sew/glue on little labels. It's the true mark of a real artist!

❀ Make a party out of the makeover madness! Invite some friends over and ask them to help you. Then do the same for them!

❀ Put some funky music or a chick flick on while you work.

❀ Most important, ask your parents before you do anything crazy!

Adventure

If the only kind of art you know comes from bouncy TV commercials, you need to be enlightened, pronto. Somewhere inside you is a colorful piñata of creativity, just waiting to be busted open. It's time to take an artsy adventure through the playground of your mind! Here are some tricks to put you on the right path. Once your crafty soul is unleashed, there'll be no stopping you!

PAINTED PAINTBRUSHES

CRAFTY DiVA

MONSTER MUSE

megan

PAPER PORTRAIT COLLAGE

Painted Paintbrushes

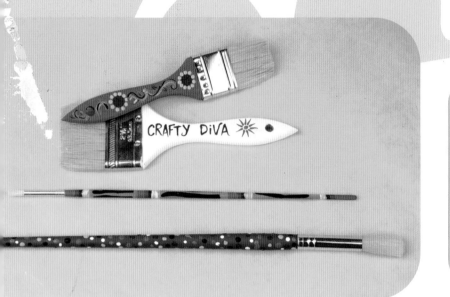

STUFF YOU'LL NEED

assorted paintbrushes with thick wooden handles

sandpaper

craft acrylic paints in assorted colors and paintbrushes (to actually paint with)

water-based varnish and brush

In order to make great-looking art, you need to put yourself in a happy, whimsical setting. You know, like with some decent tunes, a tidy workspace, and fun supplies. That last one is my favorite. Think of how much fun it will be to paint with *painted* paintbrushes. They'll look so incredibly awesome, there's no doubt they'll have special artistic powers!

How to Do It

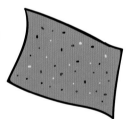

1. Lightly sand the handles of the brushes to remove the protective coating. Wipe off any dust.

2. Paint the handles of the brushes. Paint one side first so you can lay it flat to dry. Then flip it over and paint the other side. Let dry.

3. Have at it! Add all kinds of little details, working on one side at a time. Add polka dots, stripes, stars, or flowers and let dry. Flip over and do the other side.

4. Brush on the varnish (one side at a time) to seal it all in. Let dry before using.

Apply two or three layers of varnish to really seal in your hard work. Don't forget to let each layer dry (about 30 minutes) before adding the next one.

Other Ideas

❋ Use squeeze paints to add fun, bumpy accents. But be careful—this kind of paint takes longer to dry.

❋ Write your name (or other words that you like) on the handles.

❋ Instead of painting, glue pictures all over the handles. Seal by covering with a piece of clear shelf liner (otherwise the pictures will get ruined when you rinse the brushes in water).

GET INSPIRED!

When it comes to making art, the most important thing is inspiration. When you are inspired, the creative ideas pour out of you! And then there are the other times...the times when you stare at a blank piece of paper with no clue where to start. Don't you hate it when that happens? Creative blocks are perfectly normal—every artist gets them from time to time—so don't let it get you down or stop you from designing a future masterpiece. Here are some tricks to get that idea machine up and running again.

❋ Take a walk in the park or even just around the block. Look at the cars, trees, plants, and people you see. Pick up interesting objects like leaves, bottle caps, or funky-shaped rocks and think of how you can use them in your work.

❋ Ask your parents to take you to an arts festival. Stop at every booth and look at the handmade work. When you see work you like, ask the artist how he or she gets inspired to create—you might learn something!

❋ Watch home improvement or craft shows on television to get new ideas. Think about how you can make the same types of things but with your own unique twist.

❋ Go to the local library or bookstore and look at do-it-yourself books and magazines.

❋ Whenever you are shopping or watching a movie, take a close look at the decorations and accessories to see how color combinations are used.

❋ Enroll in a local art class so you can learn new techniques that you'd never thought of before.

Paper Portrait Collage

Who are you and what do you look like? Wait. Before you go peek in the mirror, close your eyes and think about it. Many times the way we *imagine* we look and the way we *really* look are two different things. In this self-portrait collage, show the way you feel inside. Feeling wild? Make your hair neon green—or any other color. When you're done, hang it on the wall to remind you of how creative you are. Make another one down the road to see how much your self-perspective has changed.

STUFF YOU'LL NEED

blank canvas board, 8 x 10 inches

assorted papers (patterned, construction, ripped-out magazine pages, etc.)

glitter, sequins, feathers, or fabric trim (optional)

letter stickers

glue stick

white glue

scissors

How to Do It

1. Look at your papers. Sort out which ones will be used for the background and which for your face, lips, eyes, cheeks, nose, hair, and eyebrows.

2. Cover the canvas board with a thin layer of white glue. Use your fingertips to spread it all around from corner to corner.

3. Apply the paper you want for the background and smooth it down, making sure to flatten any air bubbles.

4. Take the paper you want for your face. Fold it in half and cut out an oval, circle, or square (depending on the shape of face you want).

5. Now do the same with other pieces of paper to cut out shapes for your eyes, lips, and so on. Once they are all cut out, lay them on the board and arrange the face. Keep working at it until you like the way it looks.

6. With the glue stick, apply the face, followed by the eyes, nose, mouth, and cheeks. Now add the hair. Cut out very thin strips of paper to outline the eyes and add eyelashes. Make a flower for the hair or add other accessories with glitter, sequins, and trim if you want.

7. Add a funky border around the edge. Use the letter stickers to put your name at the bottom. Frame, then hang!

TIP If you make a mistake, just carefully peel up the paper before the glue dries and do it again.

Other Ideas

❋ Buy a blank book and put a self-portrait on each page. Make each one different to show how you're feeling that day.

❋ Use fabric or Fun Foam instead of paper to make a 3-D collage.

❋ Get a few smaller canvas boards and invite your best friends over to each make a self-portrait. Then hang them all together in your room.

❋ Once you become a pro, make portraits of other people and give them away as gifts.

TERRIFIC TECHNIQUES TO TRY!

The thing that makes art so much fun is that there are so many ways to do it! Check out these ideas and give them a try the next time you're feeling arty.

❋ **Tissue paper decoupage.** Cut out shapes from colored tissue paper and glue them onto a glass bottle or jar. Let dry for 30 minutes. Brush a thin layer of white glue on top and let dry again. Then add a coat of water-based varnish. When it dries it will leave a pretty, glowing, see-through effect, just like stained glass! Use the jar to hold fresh flowers or little wishes written on paper.

❋ **Instead of paint, use watercolor pencils.** Watercolor pencils are way cool. Draw your picture on watercolor paper and then go over your design with a paintbrush that's been dipped in water. It will blend all your colors together and look gorgeous!

❋ **Make little shadow boxes.** Do you love to save teeny-weeny objects, like movie ticket stubs, a loose Barbie shoe, or gumball machine toys? Put them to good use by making a little arrangement inside a shoebox lid. This is called *assemblage* art and it's super fun. Just cover the box with funky patterned paper and then use white glue to attach your little objects in a way that makes you smile. You can call it "My Favorite Little Things." Add some pictures and you'll have one nifty-looking piece of art.

Monster Muse

STUFF YOU'LL NEED

piece of paper and marker

2 pieces of felt or fake fur,
   each 8 x 11 inches

straight pins

needle and thread

small buttons

embroidery thread

pillow stuffing

chopstick or long paintbrush

scissors

Inspiration in your art is as important as milk in your Frosted Flakes. How do you get it? Many people have a "muse" to keep them inspired. A muse is a thing or person that ignites your creative fire, so that all you want to do is paint, write, draw, or sing. You won't even hear Mom calling you for dinner! These fuzzy little creatures will do the trick as your muse. Make one as adorable and wacky as you can, give it a name, and make it your new best friend. Every time you're about to get crafty, set it close by to cheer you on.

How to Do It

1. Draw a shape for your monster on a piece of paper. If you want your monster to be the same on both sides, fold the paper in half and draw half the body along the fold. (You know how you draw half a heart, cut it out, and open it so you have a full heart? This is the same idea.) You can make your monster one big blob, or you can draw an ear, arm, and leg. Cut out the shape and open the paper. This is your pattern.

2. Lay the two pieces of felt or fake fur together, right sides in. Lay the pattern on top and trace around it with the marker. Remove the pattern. Pin the two pieces of fur or fabric together in the center of the monster.

3. Cut around the outline, leaving a margin (or "halo") of about ½ inch all around the outside.

4. Use the needle and thread to sew along the marker outline, but stop when you get to the head, leaving it open. (See page 10 for how to sew by hand.) Remove the pins and turn the monster inside out. Use the chopstick to poke out tiny areas, like the arms, feet, or ears.

5. If you are sewing on buttons or other decorations for the eyes, nose, or mouth, do it now. You can also glue on wiggly eyes and lips cut out of red felt.

6. Take a handful of the pillow stuffing and squish it into the monster. Use the chopstick to poke it into the small corners. Add more until the entire monster is stiff and full.

7. Pin the opening and then sew it closed. Squish it so the pillow stuffing is even all over the body.

Other Ideas

* Sew on fringe for the hair or add trim.

* Make a whole bunch, for your very own "muse spirit squad"!

TIP You can use two pieces of felt or fur that are the same color, or use two different colors so the front of your monster is different from its back.

19

Room

CORK WALL TILES

Is your room still full of the same cutesy pillows, bunny rabbits, and tiny bunches of flowers that have been there since you were a kid? It's time for a change! Why not discover the true meaning of "crib," where only the hippest of hip will do? So what if you can't afford to rip out your carpet or buy a new bed. There are plenty of ways to add pizzazz to your palace without going broke. Let's get started!

SWEET-AND-SOUR BED PILLOW

SWEET

SNORING IN PROGRESS

HIPPIE-CHICK SHEET SET

Cork Wall Tiles

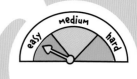

Are you the type who empties her pockets in random places? If so, here's a superstar way to get organized. The trick to decent decorating is using items that not only look like a million dollars, but also have a million uses. These cork wall tiles are sold in the office supply area in packages of four and are primed and ready to be an important part of your room redo. Hang them in a row as diamonds, edge-to-edge for a large cube, or randomly scattered. And hey! Don't forget to make pushpins to match!

STUFF YOU'LL NEED

4 cork tiles

craft acrylic paints in assorted colors and paintbrushes

fabric appliqués (these are cute, iron-on patches that you can find at the craft or fabric store)

plastic cup to hold pens

small mirror

pushpins

Crafter's Pick "The Ultimate" craft glue

sawtooth picture hangers

How to Do It

1. Give each tile a base coat of paint in any color. Let dry.

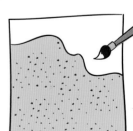

2. Decorate! Glue on the appliqués, paint on stripes and polka dots—whatever you want. Let dry.

3. Glue the mirror in the center of one tile. Glue the plastic cup in the center of another. Paint or glue on more decorations around them. Let everything dry.

4. Flip the cork tiles over and glue a sawtooth picture hanger on the back of each. Let dry.

4. Hang! And don't forget to put pens in the cup!

Other Ideas

❀ Cover the tiles with fabric or craft foam for a thicker look.

❀ Stencil a letter or word on each tile to spell out a word or phrase when you hang them.

❀ Buy a bunch of tiles and use them as a border all around the walls of your room. No matter where you are, you will always have a bulletin board nearby.

DECORATING DOS AND DON'TS

Tana March has written for *TEEN* and *Teen Beat* magazines, TEENMag.com, Seventeen.com, and HGTV's *Awesome Interiors*. Here are her tips for redoing your room in style.

❀ **What's a sure sign that is it time to redo your room?**
It's always time to redo your room! My place is in constant flux—out with the old, in with the new. And it's not always big stuff, but little things like a pillow or a wind chime. It doesn't have to be a huge ordeal. Let your room change with your personality. That way, you won't wind up with a Holly Hobbie room filled with stuffed animals and loose Barbie parts at age 17!

❀ **How do you make a small bedroom look big?**
Keep it simple. Use the same color for the walls, shades, and furniture. (This is called a *monochromatic* color scheme.) Leave patterns and accent colors for your linens, pillows, and knobs.

❀ **What are the no-nos?**

1. Clutter.

2. Picking a style that looks cool, but doesn't feel livable. Who wants an uncomfortable room?

3. Spending a ton of cash. Unless you're grounded all the time, you're probably not going to be in your room that much. Save your money for fun stuff like movies and skiing and put your noggin to work on creative decorating solutions that can be done on the cheap.

4. Fighting with your parents about painting your room black. They really do have something to say, so see if you can come to a peaceful compromise you're both happy with.

5. The color beige. Enough said.

TIPS FROM THE EXPERT

23

Hippie-Chick Sheet Set

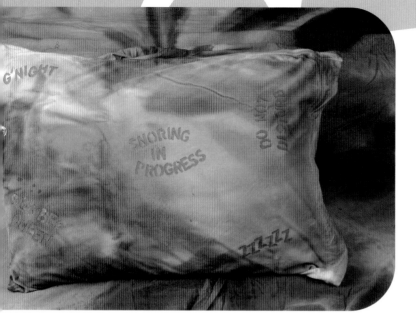

easy · medium · hard

STUFF YOU'LL NEED

sheet set (cotton or jersey knit)

craft acrylic paints in assorted colors

16-ounce plastic cups

plastic tarp (or large plastic garbage bags cut open)

letter stencils

medium paintbrush

chopstick or mixing stick

plastic gloves

spray bottle filled with water

Waaaay back in the 1960s, a little thing called "tie-dye" was all the rage. It's where you take a shirt and tie knots in it and then soak different areas in fabric dye. You open the shirt and—whoa!—you have a crazy, swirly, psychedelic design. The crafty diva knows there is more to tie-dye than shirts alone. Why not your bedsheets? Snuggling up in bed has never been so cool. It's all about peace, love, and paint, baby.

How to Do It

1. Run the sheets through the washing machine, but don't put them in the dryer.

2. Go outside and lay the plastic tarp or garbage bags on the ground. Open one of the sheets and lay it on the plastic.

3. Squeeze some paint (about two big, quick squirts) into one of the cups. Fill it with water to about an inch from the top. Stir with a chopstick. Repeat for the other colors (as many as you want).

4. Put the gloves on. Pick up one of the colors and pour a little bit on different areas of the sheet. Repeat with another color. Spray water wherever the two colors

meet so they will blend together. Continue with more colors until the entire sheet is covered.

5. Hang the sheet on an outdoor clothesline to dry. While it's drying, repeat step 4 with the other sheet, then the pillowcases.

6. When everything is dry, bring it all into the house. Use letter stencils and craft acrylic paint to add phrases like "snoring in progress," "g'night," or "dreaming diva." Let dry.

7. Rinse each sheet and pillowcase in the sink or bathtub and wring it out. This will remove any extra paint. Now run them through the washing machine (with no other clothes) on a regular cycle, then through the dryer.

LEARN FENG SHUI!

What the heck is feng shui? It sounds like the noise that comes out when you sneeze. Feng shui (pronounced fung SHWAY) is the ancient Chinese art of arranging your stuff in a way that will bring balance, harmony, and luck into your life. We all want that, right? It can be the way your stuffed animals are arranged on your bed, the colors of your room, even the thoughts that run through your head. Here are some tips on using the power of feng shui to brighten your life.

❀ Clean your room. No, really. Clean it. Get rid of any clutter under your bed, on top of your furniture, and even in that closet. Junk lying around stops the flow of positive energy.

❀ Try adding small accents with these feng shui colors:

BLUE for relaxation

YELLOW for friendship and warmth

WHITE for purity and cleanliness

ORANGE for organization and creativity

PURPLE for good health

GREEN for inner growth and spirituality

RED for good fortune and energy

❀ Move your furniture so it's spaced out, not clumped together. There should be room to move around without bumping into anything. This will keep the good energy flowing.

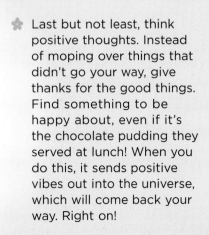

❀ Last but not least, think positive thoughts. Instead of moping over things that didn't go your way, give thanks for the good things. Find something to be happy about, even if it's the chocolate pudding they served at lunch! When you do this, it sends positive vibes out into the universe, which will come back your way. Right on!

25

Sweet-and-Sour Bed Pillow

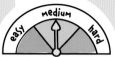

STUFF YOU'LL NEED

3 pieces of felt in different colors, each 8 x 10 inches
index card
set of glittery iron-on letters
ironing board and iron
fabric glue (optional)
straight pins
needle and thread
pillow stuffing
scissors

Those who dare enter the room of the resident princess, beware. Not knowing what kind of mood she is in can lead to painful suffering on the part of any innocent passerby. Don't let this happen to your family. They are such nice people, don't you think? Yes, even your little brother or sister. Whip up a throw pillow for your bed that shows exactly what your state of mind is before they put their lives at risk.

How to Do It

1. Take one of the pieces of felt and fold it in half. Lay the index card on top and cut around it, cutting through both layers of felt. You should end up with two little pieces of felt the same size as the index card.

2. Cut out the iron-on letters. Follow the package directions to put the word "sour" on one of the little pieces of felt, and "sweet" on the other. Trim each piece so it fits snugly around the word. If you want to add a border, dab some glue on the back

OUCH! You can get seriously burned using an iron! If you have never used an iron before, ask an adult for help or use letter stencils and paint instead.

of each piece and press it onto another piece of felt or fabric. Let dry, then cut around the smaller piece to leave a border.

3. Get the other two pieces of felt. These will be the front and back of the pillow. Sew or use fabric glue to put a word on each piece.

4. Lay the two pieces of felt together right side out, with the edges lined up evenly, and pin in place. Sew around the edges, leaving a small margin all the way around. Leave one of the short ends open. (See page 10 for tips on sewing by hand.)

5. Take out the pins. Fill with pillow stuffing until it looks fluffy. Now sew the last edge closed.

Other Ideas

❋ Add sequins, trim, or fringe.

❋ Use other words like "hello/good-bye," "friendly/grumpy," "perky/not perky," or whatever describes you best.

❋ Instead of stuffing the pillow, leave it open and hang it on your wall so people can stuff notes inside for you, or hang it on your door to show your mood.

Social

Best friends are the chocolate sprinkles on the sundae of life. From giggle-fest sleepovers to Girl Scout meetings, they make your world a wacky carnival. But while it's absolutely awesome to spend time with your crew, there's nothing wrong with meeting new people. Just like ice cream—it's good to try a new flavor! You'll never know how many lovable amigas are out there until you look beyond your current group. Take a chance and strike up a conversation with a new person every now and then. After all, there's no such thing as too many friends!

CRAZY CALLING CARDS

SLEEPOVER SUITCASE

You're-Too-Sweet Picture Frame

STUFF YOU'LL NEED

mini picture frame

craft acrylic paint

paintbrush

assorted hard candies (candy necklaces, jelly beans, bubble gum, candy hearts, mints, and so on)

Crafter's Pick "The Ultimate" craft glue

picture of your friend or crush

spray varnish

No matter what, there's always one drop-dead gorgeous guy in homeroom class who you secretly adore. Or maybe it's Ashton's face that sends your heart into a tailspin. Either way, get that yearbook or magazine, make a copy of his sweet face, and frame him in all his sugarcoated glory with one of these too-cute frames. Don't blame me if you get a toothache.

How to Do It

1. Cover the frame with a coat of paint in any color. Let dry.

2. Lay the frame face up on a flat surface. Squeeze some glue onto the frame and smooth it over the entire surface with your fingers. Wipe your fingers clean. Pick up a piece of candy and place it on the glue. (If the candies come wrapped in plastic, you can glue them on that way, too.) Repeat until the whole frame is covered with candy.

3. Take the frame outside and lightly spray with varnish. Let dry.

It's all right if you don't have spray varnish. Leave the frame out and the candies will eventually harden.

4. Insert your crush's gorgeous face, and enjoy!

Other Ideas

* Use mini beads or stickers that look like little candies instead of the real thing.

* Try gluing teeny toys all around the frame.

* If you want to use bigger items, get a bigger frame.

BE A SOCIAL DIVA!

Looking for ways to meet new friends? Try these ideas on for size.

* If you are super-duper shy, challenge yourself to say hi to one new person every day. Eventually work up to two people, and so on. Don't know what to say? Look at what they're wearing or reading and make a nice comment about it, or ask a question, like "Hey, that's a really cool Emily Strange patch. Where did you get it?" You can also mention something about school, a popular song, the meal being served for lunch, or, if all else fails, the weather!

* Join a school group like band, a sports team, or even the chess club. You'll pick up a new talent and meet people at the same time.

* Volunteer at a creative place like the local actor's theater or a crafting or book group. Or take a painting class at an arts center.

* When working on your school assignments, ask a new person to join your study group.

* Invite your new friends over for a crafting or karaoke party. Don't forget to invite your best friends, too.

* Most importantly, feel good about yourself! You make your family laugh at the dinner table and you know you can tell a killer joke. Your best friends adore you because you are faithful, funny, and oh-so-smart. So why be so chicken about meeting new people? If you get nervous, pretend you are an award-winning actress until you get comfy in your own skin. You'll be surprised at how happy people will be to meet you!

Crazy Calling Cards

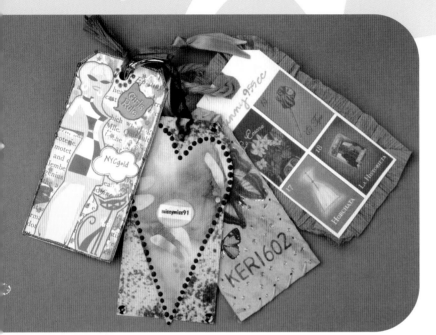

STUFF YOU'LL NEED

large luggage tags (found at the office supply store)

stickers, decorative papers, rubber stamps, and/or pictures

pens, markers, and crayons

sequins, rhinestones, gems, and micro-glitter

binder ring (found at the office supply store)

glue stick

scissors

"What's your screen name?" How often do you hear that? To stay in the loop of instant messaging, make a batch of these crazy calling cards, also known as artist trading cards. Decorate them to match your personality and show your IM screen name, then give 'em away. Invite your sidekicks to do the same, then trade them and pin them up on your bulletin board so you won't forget who to add to your online buddy list.

How to Do It

1. Smear the glue stick all over one side of the tag. Press a piece of decorative paper on it to be the background for your card. Trim off any extra paper.

2. Add the focal point of the card, like a picture, stamped image, or a phrase made with cut-out words and letters. Then add other details around it, like smaller pictures, sequins, gems, and glitter. Make the card wild, elegant, funky, or funny—whatever suits your personality. Don't limit yourself to the shape of the card; it's okay if the papers stick out beyond the edge.

3. Use a pen, letter stencil, or stickers to add your IM screen name.

4. Repeat to make more tags. When you're done, hang them all on a binder ring for safekeeping until you give them away.

TIP

If you don't have a glue stick, white glue will work fine, too.

Other Ideas

✿ Instead of luggage tags, buy a cheap deck of playing cards and decorate them for your cards. Give some to your friends to decorate, too.

✿ Tie pretty yarn or ribbon through the hole.

CRAFTING WITH FRIENDS

Petra Cuschieri, a 17-year-old from Ontario, Canada, is crafty in more ways than one. When she isn't doing her homework, she is whipping up purses, messenger bags, tote bags, and wallets that she sells through her company, Petrified Baggage. She credits her friends as a big part of her design inspiration. Here are her thoughts on getting crafty with friends.

✿ It's a great idea to craft with your friends! You can give each other ideas for new projects and clever ways of doing things.

✿ Before having a craft party, always make sure to get all the supplies you'll need.

✿ Good group projects include decorating small boxes, making funky jewelry, or revamping plain T-shirts and shoes.

✿ Never let crafts stress you out. It's meant to be FUN, so make sure it stays that way for you and your friends.

✿ If it goes well, plan on getting together once a month to make something new. Let each person take a turn picking the project.

Sleepover Suitcase

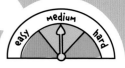

STUFF YOU'LL NEED

small suitcase with hard out-side and lid that opens from the top (can be found at the thrift store or discount department store)

1–2 packages of vintage sewing patterns

Mod Podge and foam brush

feather boa

old cloth measuring tape

assorted buttons

3-D squeeze paint

water-based varnish and foam brush

Crafter's Pick "The Ultimate" craft glue

scissors

Whether it's a slumber party with the whole crew or just a regular old sleepover with your best bud, show up in style and you'll make all the more impact. This ultra-funkadelic sleepover suitcase has plenty of room for your pj's and toothbrush, plus secret surprises like makeup, craft supplies, magazines, or better yet, gourmet chocolate bars. I mean, no one's planning to *sleep*, are they?

How to Do It

1. Open the suitcase and see if it needs to be cleaned out. Wipe clean and let dry.

2. Use the foam brush to paint a layer of Mod Podge all over the lid of the case. Open up the sewing patterns and lay them on the wet surface. Use the foam brush to smooth out the wrinkles. Make sure to keep the straight edges lined up with the edges of the case, so you won't have to worry about paper going over the sides. Let dry, then add another layer of paper.

TIP

Let each layer of Mod Podge dry completely (about 20 minutes) before applying the next.

6. Add a line of craft glue along the lip of the lid, just above the metal edging. Place the measuring tape over the glue. When you get to the corners, snip them so they will lie flat. Run your fingers over the tape so it will stay in place.
Let dry.

3. Repeat for the bottom part of the suitcase. Since the patterns are so thin, it may take a few layers to cover up the color of the case.

4. Cut out the pictures of the girls from the front of the pattern packages. Use the Mod Podge and foam brush to stick them to the top, sides, and front of the case at whatever angles you like. Let dry. Outline the girls with 3-D squeeze paint. Let dry.

7. Run a line of glue along one of the upper ridges of the bottom part of the case and apply the boa all the way around. Let dry.

5. Use a foam brush to apply a coat of varnish all over the case. Let dry.

8. Fill it up with stuff and head out to have fun!

Other Ideas

✿ Instead of using it as a sleep-over suitcase, use it as a tote for your craft supplies.

✿ Cover the whole case with fabric or fake fur, or paint it.

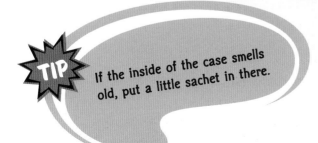

TIP

If the inside of the case smells old, put a little sachet in there.

Words

You are one smart girlie, with lots of opinions, feelings, thoughts, and dreams swirling around in your noggin. Just like the hard drive on a computer, it's time to free up some space! Let your feelings and imagination flow out by keeping a diary or writing a short story or poem. Write about what happened at school, a secret crush, places you want to go, art projects you want to make, or people you would like to meet. Listen to conversations around you and pick out words you like, then use them in your writing. Better yet, make up your own words!

RAINBOW RIBBON JOURNAL

GREETING CARD BOOKS

PICTURE PERFECT PENS

Rainbow Ribbon Journal

It's weird to think that a blank book could be your favorite accessory, even over your brand-new baby-blue iPod. But, really, it can be. Pick up a hardcover blank book and let it be your path to self-discovery. Yah, you could call it a diary, but doesn't "journal" sound so much more interesting?

STUFF YOU'LL NEED

blank book with hard cover

3–4 spools of ribbon in different colors and textures

Crafter's Pick "The Ultimate" craft glue

scissors

TIP Don't use ribbons that are loosely woven—they won't look as good after they're glued.

How to Do It

1. Decide how you want the ribbons to be arranged on the cover. Play around until you like the design.

2. Squeeze a very thin line of glue along the bottom of the front cover. Unwrap one of the spools and place the ribbon on the glue, leaving a fingernail's width hanging over the edge. Smooth the ribbon down with your fingers. Cut the other end off when you get to the spine. Continue with the other ribbons, gluing down one at a time.

3. After you've covered the entire front surface, open the cover. Add a dab of glue to the end of each ribbon and fold it over onto the inside of the cover. Close the book so the ribbons will dry flat.

Other Ideas

* To make the ribbon go all the way around from the front cover to the back, just add the glue all the way across the book. The spine area is a little tricky, so take your time.

* Instead of ribbon, cut up strips of fabric.

Picture Perfect Pens

easy medium hard

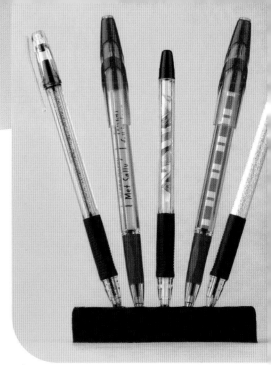

These cool personalized pens will give you the inspiration you need for writing adventures in your journal. You can slide in secret notes, pictures of friends, even micro-fine glitter. Your desk neighbor will be so impressed! Buy a whole pack, do them all, and pass them out like candy.

STUFF YOU'LL NEED

package of clear plastic pens with removable ends

very thin paper or pictures cut into 1- x 3-inch strips

chopstick

TIP Stay away from really thick paper because it won't fit in the casing. And be careful when handling the ink stem. You don't want to break it open—trust me!

How to Do It

1. Unscrew or pull out the tip of the pen and remove the ink stem (the thin tube full of ink).

2. Take the paper and roll it tightly around the ink stem.

3. Carefully put the covered ink stem back into the casing. If it doesn't fit, roll the paper tighter. You may have to trim some extra paper off as each brand of pen is slightly different.

4. Use the chopstick to gently push the paper down the inside of the casing. Screw the tip of the pen back on.

Other Ideas

* Use the pens to advertise your web site by sliding in a paper with your web address.

* Print out your favorite quotes on the computer and use those.

* Instead of using paper, remove the end of the pen and squirt in some micro-fine glitter for a shimmery look.

DEAR DIARY...

Personal journals are priceless. They help you keep track of who you are, what you're thinking, and how you've changed. When you're stressed or angry, writing in a journal can help calm you down. When you're happy, it's a place to record your thoughts so you can look back on them later and smile. It's a place to write secrets and laugh about stuff you wouldn't dare share with anyone else.

Maybe you're new to this whole diary thing, or maybe you're an old hand who's fallen into a rut—either way, here are some fun exercises to get your writing juices flowing.

ROUND ONE

Rewrite the sentences below in your journal, filling in the blanks as you go.

1. If I could be invisible for one day I would SO love to _____.

2. _____ makes my heart beat so fast that I just want to go and do something crazy, like _____ _____!!!

3. The last time I laughed so hard that my drink came out of my nose was when _____.

4. If I could trade places with a celebrity for one day, it would be _____ so I could _____.

5. _____ always makes me cry like a baby. Maybe it's because _____ _____.

6. I really want to try to stop _____ and learn how to _____.

7. If I had the guts, I would like to _____ _____.

8. The most embarrassing moment in my life was when _____.

9. I really kick butt at _____.

10. If I could star in my own movie, it would be called _____ and it would be about a girl who _____.

TIP

There's no better way to become a better writer than keeping a journal or notebook. Sit down once a day and just start writing (without thinking hard about *what* you're writing). Let your mind wander. Sometimes you can get your greatest inspirations that way. Remember, good writing takes practice, practice, practice. The more you write, the better you will become.

ROUND TWO

Look at each pair below and circle the one you like best. Don't stop and think about it—just do it really fast! When you're done, look back at what you circled. Did you learn anything new about yourself? If so, write about it in your journal.

1. Fashion model or fashion designer
2. Orange juice or orange pants
3. Handwritten or typed
4. Home run or homebody
5. Mall or market
6. Marker or crayon
7. Rock collector or rock star
8. Jessica or Ashlee
9. Face or phone
10. Scrabble or Mario Party
11. Hot pink or baby blue
12. Heels or sneakers
13. Chocolate lip gloss or chocolate fudge

ROUND THREE

Favorites! Copy the list below in your journal and write in your answers. Think of it as a written time capsule of this very moment in your life. Years later, you'll look back and say, "I can't believe I said that!"

1. Favorite piece of clothing I own:
2. Favorite CD:
3. Favorite TV show:
4. Crush at school:
5. Fantasy crush:
6. Best friend:
7. Favorite junk food:
8. Worst bad habit:
9. Favorite phrase I like to say:
10. Favorite class and teacher:
11. Favorite movie:

Greeting Card Books

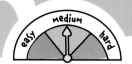

Now that you've been bitten by the writing bug, do your friends a favor and turn them on to it, too! These cute little page-turners will do the trick. Whip up a few, pass them out, and have everyone write a mini-novel, comic series, movie review, or silly poem inside. Then trade them with each other and enjoy!

STUFF YOU'LL NEED

greeting card and envelope

4 sheets of blank paper (typing, construction, stationery, or handmade)

hole punch and soft ribbon OR large needle and embroidery thread

pencil

scissors

How to Do It

1. Put the papers in a neat stack. Open the card and lay it flat on top. Trace around the card with a pencil, then cut around the outline. You should end up with four pieces of paper the same size as the open card.

2. Fold the sheets of paper in half to make the pages. Run the edge of a ruler over the fold to make it crisp all the way down. This will make the book lie flat.

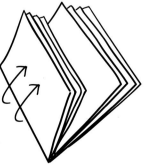

3. Insert the pages in the card. Trim off any extra paper that sticks out when the card is closed.

4. Punch holes at the top and bottom of the booklet, along the crease. Push one end of the ribbon through each hole from the inside and tie in a bow. If you are using a needle and thread, do the same process.

5. Slide your book inside the envelope until it is time to use it.

TIP Don't use more than four sheets paper because it will make the holes rip when you close the book.

Other Ideas

❀ Liven up the front of the book by coloring in areas with squeeze paint or gluing on micro-glitter.

❀ Decorate the envelope to match.

❀ Buy a box of cards and make each into a little book. Then put the books back in the box and give it as a gift.

❀ Attach the books to other gifts.

START YOUR OWN ZINE

What the heck is a "zine"? A zine is a self-published booklet. It can be written as a journal, a travel log, or a how-to book, like a cookbook. Karen Sawicki of New Jersey is only 16 and she is already a pro at producing her own line of zines, which she sells online and to friends. Here are her tips on getting your own zine started.

❀ To make a zine, all you need is a photocopier, paper, stapler, glue sticks, scissors, and photos or images from magazines to cut up.

❀ Start by choosing a simple topic for your zine. It's very important to pick something you know about. It could be a lighthearted look at your life, a guide to making the best brownies—whatever. Just make sure it's something you feel comfortable writing about.

❀ Create the pages by cutting and pasting pictures and words onto the paper.

❀ When you're done, photocopy the pages to make as many zines as you want. Staple each in the center. My first zine was an itty-bitty 20 pages. My latest one is a whopping 64!

❀ Listen to music as you work to keep you going!

TIPS FROM THE EXPERT

for Fashion

Your closet's contents may be about as exciting as your grandpa's, but girl, there is a red carpet out there waiting for you to glide down it, and time's a-wastin'! It doesn't matter if you just want to wear clothes or design them, it's smart to know a little bit about clothing composition and fashion design. Consider this your head start.

SKINNY SCARF

HAPPY HANGERS

Cut-and-Paste Tee

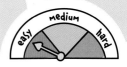

T-shirts are one of the joys of life—it doesn't matter how old you are or what your style. But what happens when you outgrow that beloved old-school Minnie Mouse tee? Give it to the garment graveyard? I think not! Read on to see how you can salvage it and turn it into the next best (or better) thing.

How to Do It

1. Wash and iron both shirts so they are crisp and wrinkle-free.

2. Cut out the design from the old shirt, leaving a wide border around it.

3. Lay the design face down on a flat surface. Add a line of fabric glue around the edges and fold them over to make a nice hem. Let dry.

STUFF YOU'LL NEED

old T-shirt to cut up
new T-shirt
decorative trim
3-D squeeze paint
straight pins
fabric glue
scissors

TIP

If you're handy with a sewing machine, feel free to skip the fabric glue.

Other Ideas

❋ Glue the design onto a piece of far-out looking fabric before gluing it onto the T-shirt.

❋ Use the same process to add an old T-shirt design to a canvas tote bag or a toss pillow.

❋ Instead of using one big design, cut out letters from old shirts and arrange them on a new shirt to spell out quirky sayings.

4. Lay the new shirt flat on a table, face up. Think about how you want to place the design. Straight or crooked? In the center or on the side? Move it around until you like the way it looks.

5. Once you've decided, apply fabric glue to the back of the design. Spread it around evenly and generously, then wipe off your fingers. Carefully turn the design over and place it on the new shirt. Smooth it down with your fingers. Add another thin line of glue right under the edges and press them down so they are secure.

6. Using the fabric glue, add some trim around the border of the design. To make it really stand out, add a border of dots with the 3-D squeeze paint. Let dry. When it comes time to wash your tee, use the gentle cycle.

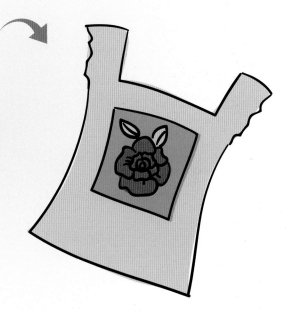

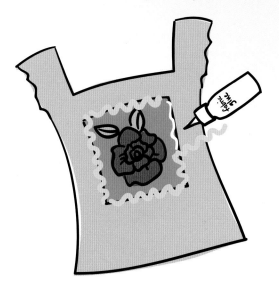

TIP

If you wear out the new shirt, make a gym bag out of it! See pages 66–67 to find out how.

Happy Hangers

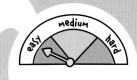

Whether your closet is full of the trendiest of trendy ensembles or just a ratty pair of overalls and a poncho you knitted in Home Ec, it's time to celebrate your threads! Top-notch clothes deserve top-notch hangers. With a little help from some fuzzy pipe cleaners, your clothes will be treated like the shining stars they are.

STUFF YOU'LL NEED

plastic hanger

bag of pipe cleaners

fake flowers with leaves
  (found at the craft store)

Crafter's Pick "The Ultimate"
  craft glue

clothespins

How to Do It

1. Take a pipe cleaner and hold it tightly against the hanger with your finger. Use your other hand to wrap the pipe cleaner around the hanger, moving along the hanger as you go.

2. When you get to the end of the pipe cleaner, leave a tiny tail and twist it to the start of the next pipe cleaner. This will make the wrapping look nice and even.

3. Continue wrapping pipe cleaners around the entire hanger.

4. When you're done, run your fingers over the hanger to feel for any edges poking out. If you find any, press them under a wrapped pipe cleaner. You don't want them to catch on your clothes!

5. Glue the leaves and flowers to the neck area of the hanger. Use a clothespin to hold them in place until dry.

TIP Don't use silver tinsel for this project. It looks really neat and disco-y, but it will snag your clothes for sure. Mmmmkay!

Other Ideas

* Instead of attaching a flower, hang a little sachet on the hanger and put it at the back of your closet to keep it smelling fresh.

* If you don't have pipe cleaners, use thick yarn instead.

BE A FASHION DESIGNER

Stephanie Rasmussen, of Milwaukee, Wisconsin, began sewing her own clothes when she was only 9 years old. Now, at 21, she runs her own online boutique, Urban Ophelia. Here are her tips for getting on the inside track to becoming a clothing designer.

* Do research. Look through magazines to find new trends and styles you like. Spend time at fabric stores to get a feel for what's out there. Find a designer you can spend a few hours with to see how he or she "does it."

* Get a head start by taking sewing and fashion design courses at your school or a local fabric store.

* Practice! Try making clothes better by adding your own decorations, then wear your pieces to see what kind of response you get.

* Once you've made a bunch of things, invite some friends over to try them on. Seeing the clothes on someone else may make it easier to see how they should be changed.

* Always add labels to your finished pieces. It's an important way of marketing your creations. Even if it is only you wearing it,

think of how professional it will look to have a label with your name on it.

* Once you have your designs tested and ready to roll, take pictures that you can put online. Come up with a catchy name for your business and ask your parents if you can make a small web site to show your work.

* Do a web search to find other young designers and see if they want to trade links with you.

* Ask your favorite boutique owner if you can hold a trunk show there. A trunk show is where you set up your pieces and invite people to come see them—you may even sell something!

* If you plan to sell your items, research the price tags of other crafters. Keep track of the materials you buy and how much time you spend. Decide who you're targeting and how much they'll be willing to spend.

* Creating a wardrobe from scratch can be a sweaty deed. It takes hard work and problem solving, but to see it completed is fulfilling!

TIPS FROM THE EXPERT

49

Skinny Scarf

Not everyone lives in a snowy place, but people everywhere love to flaunt gorgeous scarves around their necks. In that case, it's time to add some nifty needlework to an otherwise boring scarf. You'll want to toss this idea over your shoulder, no matter what the temperature!

STUFF YOU'LL NEED

long, skinny scarf (can be crocheted, knitted, chenille, silk, or any soft fabric)

bag of small glass beads that go with the scarf's color scheme

needle and thread

scissors

How to Do It

1. Cut off a piece of thread 24 inches long. Thread it through the needle, leaving one end short and one end long.

2. Find an area around the top of the scarf. Poke the needle through from the back side and pull it until you have just a few inches of thread left sticking out the back. Slide a bead onto the needle and pull it down until it is resting against the scarf.

3. Bring the needle over the bead and back down through the fabric.

4. Flip the scarf over and cut the thread, leaving a 2-inch tail. Tie the two strands together so the bead won't come off. Trim the ends to neaten.

5. Repeat steps 2–4, adding more beads all over the front of the scarf in a random but balanced design.

6. Sew more beads along the ends of the scarf to give it a finished look.

Other Ideas

❋ Make scarves to match your outfits.

❋ Glue or sew fringe onto the ends.

❋ Check with local craft or yarn stores and enroll in a knitting or crochet class. Then make your own scarf to decorate!

SHAKE UP YOUR LOOK!

Here are some tips on throwin' together a whole new look. These are all hot styles that are sure to get you noticed. Check out your local mall for funky accessories to match.

❋ **Geek chic** Wear a short, plaid skirt with a button-up blouse and cardigan sweater. Stick two or three sparkly pins in a cluster on the front of your sweater or blouse. Add a simple headband, charm bracelet, knee socks, and a pair of Mary Janes or loafers. Finish with a small, old-fashioned looking purse.

❋ **Rocker raven** Start with a dark denim skirt or jeans with flared legs. Add striped stockings, black boots, and a punker T-shirt (look in local record stores). Wear chunky black and silver accessories, like a belt, bracelets, lots of rings, earrings, choker necklace, and nail polish. Wrap a super-long skinny scarf around your neck for that extra edgy touch.

❋ **Glam girl** Hot pink. Need I say more? Look for sweaters, coats, and purses with fur trim. Go for perky hats and rhinestone jewelry. Wear your hair up, just like a movie star. Don't be shy—pick up a feather boa and sling it around your bod! Dab a bit of pink body glitter on your cheeks and add a little tiara and a pair of sunglasses, too.

❋ **Retro cool** The '80s are back and we're lovin' it. This is the one time when you actually *want* to wear clashing bright colors. Layer a short-sleeved shirt over a long-sleeved one, and a skirt over stockings. Wear a jean jacket with gobs of mini music pins. Put your hair in a ponytail on top of your head. Add long, dangly earrings and tons of other jewelry. Don't forget your headphones.

❋ **Hippie chick** Wear your favorite T-shirt over a pair of corduroy jeans or flowing skirt, then add a crocheted poncho. Add a hemp choker and ankle bracelet. Let your hair fall naturally around your face and put a fresh flower behind your ear.

Inner Princess

OH OH OATMEAL MASK

We all have our not-so-great moments, whether it's an "Oh my gawd!" grade on a test or just a bad hair day. When your day becomes more gray than gold, perk up by indulging in a little movie-star treatment! Pampering your inner princess is all about tapping into the little luxuries we usually overlook—good for your mind, body, and soul. Before you know it, you'll have forgotten what got you in a bad mood to begin with. Let the spoiling begin!

HER ROYAL HIGHNESS TIARA

PEPPERMINT PICK-ME-UP FACE MIST

Oh Oh Oatmeal Mask

Give yourself a relaxing facial with good old-fashioned breakfast food. Oatmeal isn't only good with brown sugar, it's also well known for its ability to remove excess oil and relieve embarrassing pimples. When zits crop up, it's oatmeal to the rescue! This recipe includes a unique twist and also has the bonus of taming those awful, unsightly pores.

STUFF YOU'LL NEED

2 tablespoons cooked oatmeal (regular or instant)

2 teaspoons honey

1 egg white

small bowl and spoon

small empty jar with lid (optional)

How to Do It

1. Put the oatmeal and honey in the bowl. Carefully crack the egg open in two halves. Move the egg yolk between the two shells, letting the egg white drip over the sides into the bowl. Throw the yolk away.

2. Stir the mixture until it becomes a thick paste, like brownie batter. Don't eat it!

TIP

If you're storing leftover mask or giving it away as a gift, put it in a sealed container and keep it in the fridge for no longer than five days. After that it should be thrown away.

3. Wash and dry your face and pat the mixture all over. Grab a magazine to read for 15 minutes while the mask goes to work on your skin. After 15 minutes, wash it off with cool water and pat dry.

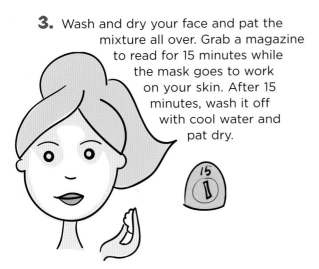

Other Ideas

❋ This recipe makes enough for one mask. Double the amount and put the extra in a pretty jar to give as a gift (or to keep for yourself!). Ask Mom for a leftover makeup jar and wash it in warm, soapy water, then let dry. Decorate the outside with stickers, put the mixture inside, and voilà—your own line of boutique skin products!

❋ Next time you have a sleepover party, make a big batch so you will all have glowing skin.

PAMPER YOUR MOOD

Feeling blah? Lara Piu of Scottsdale, Arizona, writes about beauty, spas, and spirit for her local newspaper. Her job is to test out all kinds of ways to soften our edges and calm our senses. Here are some of her secret finds.

❋ No matter what kind of day it is—a great hair day or a sick-as-a-dog day— a girl will always feel like a princess if she accepts and celebrates who she is. Embrace everything about yourself— and that means *everything,* even the not-so-perfect parts.

❋ Relax after a stressful day by treating your tootsies to a hot soak in the tub or by sitting down and doing nothing but taking deep breaths.

❋ Use crafting as a way to do something positive. Create something that makes you (and others) happy.

❋ Fill up the bathroom sink with very hot tap water, then drop an herbal tea bag in the water. Put a towel over your head and bend over the sink. The steam will get the gook out of your face and drain all your stress away, too.

❋ Pour some Epsom salts in a hot bath for a soothing getaway.

❋ Combine sea salt with olive oil for a quick and scrumptious body scrub.

TIPS FROM THE EXPERT

Peppermint Pick-Me-Up Face Mist

easy • medium • hard

When you're in need of a midday refresher (especially after a big lunch), this all-natural, breezy body spray is just what the doctor ordered. If you have super-oily skin, you'll be happy to know it also works wonders as a toner. The peppermint closes pores and helps rebalance your skin. Plus, it smells yummy, too.

How to Do It

1. Fill up a mug with the hot water (careful!). Put the tea bag inside and let it "steep" for 15 minutes.

2. Decorate the spray bottle with a colorful label or glittery squeeze paints.

3. Once the hot water has cooled, remove the tea bag. Add the witch hazel and lemon juice. Stir with a spoon.

STUFF YOU'LL NEED

peppermint tea bag

1 cup boiling water

¼ cup witch hazel (found at the beauty supply store)

1 tablespoon lemon juice

plastic spray bottle

colorful label or squeeze-on glitter paints (optional)

TIP

Always put a label on the bottle so no one will mistake it for something else (like a drink!).

4. Pour it into the spray bottle and set in the fridge so it will be nice and chilly when you go to use it.

TIP

Make a batch before you go to bed so it will be chilled by morning. Always wash and dry the bottle before you fill it up again.

Other Ideas

* Take a bottle with you when you go to basketball practice to wake you up in between scoring points.

* Tie a peppermint stick onto the neck of the bottle and give it as a holiday gift.

* Buy tiny spritz bottles in the travel section of the grocery store so you can fill some up to go.

SPA SIPPER

This drink is served at top resorts and spas to soothe pampered patrons, but you can mix up your own batch right at home.

pretty pitcher and glass mugs
1 orange
1 lemon
water
sprig of washed mint

Put the mugs in the freezer so they will get nice and frosty. Fill the pitcher halfway with water. Slice up the orange and lemon and drop the slices into the pitcher. Add the sprig of mint. Put the pitcher in the freezer and let it sit for 15 minutes. Take everything out and pour some into the frosty mugs. Sip and smile. Life is good.

RECIPE

Her Royal Highness Tiara

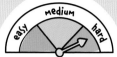

STUFF YOU'LL NEED

necklace memory wire
20 medium-sized glass beads
10–12 small glass beads
6 large glass beads
roll of 24-gauge wire
needle-nose pliers

Do you often feel like Cinderella before the ball? Don't you think you deserve a sparkly crown to wear upon your beautiful head of luscious locks? It doesn't mean you get to throw out commands like "Fetch me a decaf soy grande latte, *pronto!*" But it will add a noticeable dash of elegance to your outfit, so people will gladly *offer* you a decaf soy grande latte. This project is a real stunner, don't you think? It takes a little work, but is so totally worth it.

How to Do It

1. Cut off ¾ of one ring of the memory wire. This will be the base of the tiara that sits on your head. Use the needle-nose pliers to bend one end of the wire into a tiny loop (to keep the beads from sliding off).

2. Slide the beads onto the wire in whatever pattern you want. Leave about ½ inch at the end without any beads. Use the pliers to bend the other end into a tiny loop.

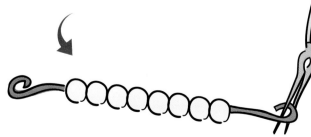

TIP

Make sure all the wire ends are crimped down nice and tight so your hair won't catch in them.

Other Ideas

❀ Glass beads can be expensive. For a cheaper version, use plastic beads instead.

❀ Add dangling charms inside the curves.

❀ Use different colored beads, or make your own beads out of oven-bake clay.

❀ If you have leftover beads, use them to make stretchy bracelets (see page 112 for instructions).

3. Now start making the arches for the top. Cut a 3-inch piece of wire and hold one end against the base, about ¼ inch in. Use the needle-nose pliers to bend the end of the wire around the base and crimp it in place.

4. Slide on one small bead, one large bead, and another small bead. Bend the wire into a curve so the large bead is at the top. Then use the pliers to bend the other end around the base of the tiara. Crimp it in place and snip off any extra wire.

5. Continue making arches all the way around. This will give you a tiara like the clear one in the photo opposite.

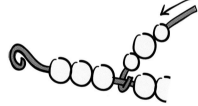

To make a taller tiara, like the colored one in the photo, just make the arches bigger, then add a third arch on top. Or make your own unique design!

Your Workout

You may not be a superstar athlete—at least not yet—but that doesn't mean you can't look good trying! There are plenty of ways to cross the finish line with a savvy sense of style. When you look good, you feel good. Before you know it, you'll be kicking, running, batting, and shooting better than ever before. Here are three sporty and spiffy ways to work it, girl.

SPORT SHIRT GYM BAG

GIRL POWER MESSAGE SOAPS

Team Spirit Hair Holders

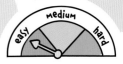

You don't have to be a perky cheer-leader to show your school spirit. Who likes somersaults and cartwheels, anyway? Well, they are kinda fun. Anyhoo—show your true colors with these bouncy and breathtaking ponytail holders. They are super-duper easy, but take a long time. So pop in a DVD of *Bring It On* and get to work.

STUFF YOU'LL NEED

hair elastics
2 spools of ribbon
scissors

How to Do It

1. Cut both spools of ribbon into strands measuring 3 inches each.

2. Take one strand and tie it onto the hair elastic.

3. Continue tying on strands and alternating colors until the entire hair elastic is covered.

4. Trim the ends so everything looks even.

TIP If you want to make a lot of these, get your whole team together and have an after-school get-together. If you don't play sports, make some in your favorite colors, just because.

Other Ideas

* Make bolder blocks of color by alternating in strands of five.

* Use fancier ribbon, like organza or silk.

* Add a few charms by attaching a small jump ring to the ribbon and connecting a dangling charm.

SPORTING IN STYLE

Don't stop here—there are all kinds of ways to craft up your sports accessories! Try these on for size.

* Embroider your initials onto a set of fuzzy wristbands.

* Take a paintbrush to your softball, bicycle, or roller-blading helmet. Use a marker to sketch out the design and then paint it on. Brush a layer of varnish on top to seal it in.

* Tired of your uniform sleeves making you all gross and sweaty? Get them out of the way by painting some small barrettes and using them as sleeve clips. Pull the bottom of the sleeve up to the neckline and clip in place.

* Cut up pictures from a skateboarding magazine and glue them all over the top of your skateboard. Brush a thick coat of varnish on top to seal them in. While you're at it, paint the outside area of your skateboard or roller blade wheels, too.

* Buy a basket for your bike and glue fake flowers all over it.

* Wrap ribbons around the handlebars of your bike and let them hang down like streamers.

* Do some crazy coloring on the rubber area of your sneakers with permanent markers.

* Paint your tennis racket in your favorite color.

* Have your team make a set of trading cards with their pictures on them (see page 32 for directions).

* Use fabric paints to add flair to a boring visor.

* Decorate a blank book so you can write down your record-breaking scores.

* Cover a large water jug with your favorite sports stickers and then bring it to the game.

* Sew crazy patches onto your leg or elbow guards.

Girl Power Message Soaps

STUFF YOU'LL NEED

melt-and-pour soap

soap coloring (optional)

plastic soap mold for individual soaps

words or phrases printed on the computer or cut from a magazine (small enough to fit in the mold, but large enough so you can see them through the soap)

decorative paper (optional)

glue stick

self-laminating sheets

rubbing alcohol in a small spray bottle

plastic bowl

knife

chopstick

scissors

To play your best, you have to feel your best. When it comes time for that championship showdown, you'll need more prepping than just regular old sweaty practice. You have to feel it in your soul, and on your bod, too. These girl power word soaps will massage your spirit to the tune of WIN! WIN! WIN! And if you don't win, at least you'll smell nice.

How to Do It

1. Cut out the phrase. If you want, use the glue stick to paste it to a piece of pretty paper. Trim the paper, leaving a border around your phrase.

2. Insert the paper in the laminating sheet and seal. Use your fingers to smooth out any air bubbles. Cut around the shape, leaving a ⅛-inch border all around it. Press the sides together firmly with your finger. If there are still little openings, use a thin piece of clear packing tape to seal the edges shut.

3. Cut off 8 cubes of the soap—this will make 3 bars. Cut them along the scored lines.

OUCH! I know you know, but I'm telling you anyway: Always use extreme caution when working with the microwave. Just like on the playing field, it's no fun to get burned!

4. Put the cubes in a plastic bowl. Heat on high in the microwave for 30 seconds. Take it out and stir with the chopstick. Keep heating for 30 seconds at a time until the soap is melted. If you want the soap tinted, squeeze in a couple drops of soap coloring and stir.

5. Pour a thin layer of melted soap into three of the molds. There should be about ¼ inch of soap in each. Spray with the

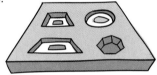

rubbing alcohol to pop the bubbles. Carefully lay a laminated message face down in the center of each. Don't move it or your soap will get cloudy.

6. Fill the molds to the top with the rest of the melted soap. Let them set for 30 minutes until they are firm. Pop the soaps from the molds. Wrap them in plastic wrap and slap a sassy sticker on the bottom.

BE A GOOD SPORT

Ready to break a sweat? Before you strap on your gear, here are some reminders.

❁ Try on your gear at the start of each season to make sure it still fits. Chances are you've outgrown some of it and may need to upgrade.

❁ Don't forget to take a little survival kit with you: water, lip balm, sunscreen, tissues, Band-Aids.

❁ Always warm up with some stretches first, to limber up your bod!

❁ If you are riding your bike or power walking, take a gal pal along. All that chatting will make the trip go faster!

❁ Exercise at the same time every day. It will become part of your daily routine and you'll stay on track.

❁ Don't let yourself get bored. There are gobs of ways to get physical—try them all and then rotate them to keep things exciting.

❁ Remember, working out is about having fun and being healthy. Don't go overboard and try to act like an Olympic contender. You have all the time in the world to build up your strength.

65

Sport Shirt Gym Bag

Over the years, you've played on so many teams that your old uniform shirts are piling up. You could donate them to a secondhand store, use them as dust rags, or lock them away as treasured mementos of your childhood. But why not do something useful with them instead and make a gym tote? Here's how.

STUFF YOU'LL NEED

sport team shirt
needle and thread
straight pins
scissors

How to Do It

1. Cut off the bottom half of the shirt from the waist area down. Now cut the up the sides to remove the sleeves and the seams. Then cut open the shoulder seams so you have two pieces. Make sure the logo is centered before you cut.

2. Lay the two pieces together inside out and pin in place. Sew down one side, across the bottom, and up the other side. If you are hand sewing, do it again so your bag will be very sturdy. (See page 10 for tips on sewing by hand.) Remove the pins.

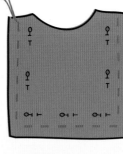

3. Turn the bag right side out. Fold the raw shoulder seams over and pin in place to make a nice, clean hem. Sew in place and remove the pins.

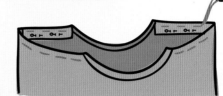

4. Get the bottom half of the shirt that you cut off in step 1. Cut it up one side to make one long strip. This will be the strap of the bag.

5. Lay the strip out flat and fold it in half lengthwise. Tuck in the raw edges and pin as you go until you've reached the end. Sew in place and remove the pins. You will end up with a smooth strap.

6. Turn the bag inside out again. Pin one end of the strap to the side seam and sew a square so it will be secure when you carry heavy items. Repeat for the other side. Turn your bag right side out and put it to good use.

Other Ideas

❋ Make pillows for your bed out of your favorite shirts.

❋ Make a larger bag by sewing several shirts together.

❋ Use cut-off pockets to make little pouches to carry lip balm, hair ties, or your school badge.

❋ Sew on your favorite patches.

TIP

Use the bag to carry things like a change of clothing, a towel, sunglasses, or a pair of sneakers. Don't put in heavy-duty stuff like a basketball or roller blades, alrighty!

Accessories

POWER-TO-THE-FLOWER HAIR CLIPS

If "high voltage" is the opposite of your style, then this is the chapter for you. It's time to transform yourself from shy girl to fly girl! Break out of your shell and ease into the center ring by using one of these show-stopping notions. One look at these and everyone on the block will ask, "Where'd ya get that?" And by that point, you'll have worked up the courage to brag about your hot handiwork.

DUCT TAPE ROSES

BEJEWELED HANDBAG PHONE

Power-to-the-Flower
Hair Clips

Flowers come in all shapes and sizes and are fresh, funky, and absolutely fabulous to wear—especially when they are attached to your hair! Super-size or extra tiny, any kind of perky petals will give new meaning to the term "flower power."

How to Do It

1. Use scissors to snip the leaves off the stems. Squeeze a line of glue along the top of the barrette and arrange the leaves in a natural fashion so they cover the top. Let dry.

STUFF YOU'LL NEED

plain metal barrettes
fake flower(s)
small fake green leaves
Crafter's Pick "The Ultimate" craft glue
blue painter's tape
scissors

TIP

Don't skip the leaf step. If you try gluing flowers directly onto metal barrettes, they will just slide off. The leaves help the flowers stay on.

2. Pull the flower off its stem. Cut any extra plastic off the flower's bottom. Add a thick drop of glue on top of the leaves and set the flower on top. Use painter's tape to hold the flower in place until dry.

3. Repeat for more barrettes.

Other Ideas

❊ Use a large single flower, a couple of medium flowers, or a row of small flowers.

❊ Glue a safety pin to the bottom of a big flower to make a pin for your coat or backpack.

❊ Add sparkle to your flowers by spritzing them with spray glitter or by gluing on tiny rhinestones.

WHERE'D YOU GET THEM SHADES?

When you hear that phrase, you know you picked the right sunglasses. But not everyone has a knack for frames. Here's all you need to know to pick out your perfect pair.

❊ The trick is to pick the right shades for your face shape.

If your face is...	your glasses should be...
OVAL	You're lucky—everything will look great on you!
ROUND	Rectangular or angular
SQUARE	Oval, cat-eye, or round
OBLONG	Square or round
HEART-SHAPED	Cat-eye or rectangular

❊ Always pick a set of frames that are the *opposite* of the shape of your face. Think of it this way: if you have a round face and choose round frames, how do you think your face will look? Round, of course!

❊ Make sure your glasses are as wide as your face, not too huge and not too tiny. Just right.

❊ Choose a pair that you love and will want to wear, so it won't end up at the bottom of your junk drawer.

❊ Clean your glasses with your fingertips and water. Dry with a soft cloth, not a paper towel or tissue, because they will scratch the lenses.

❊ Keep your shades in a carrying case for extra protection.

Bejeweled Handbag Phone

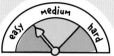

STUFF YOU'LL NEED

handbag phone (can be found at discount department stores)

3 gross (or about 400 pieces) clear acrylic gems, 7mm

Crafter's Pick "The Ultimate" craft glue

paper plate

chopstick

tweezers

In the la-la land of Beverly Hills, crystal-covered *anything* will run you hundreds—even thousands—of dollars. And that's just for a miniature cell phone! No way, Madame Makeover. It's time to liven up your favorite accessory of all time: the phone. Now if only your conversations could be as glamorous!

How to Do It

1. Remove all the cords from the phone. You will start by working on the base, so put the handset aside for now.

2. The idea is to glue on the gems in a circular pattern, following the shape of the phone. Squirt a glob of glue onto the paper plate. Dip one end of the chopstick in the glue and dab it on the phone, starting at the top edge. Pick up a gem with the tweezers and drop it onto the dot of glue.

TIP

Don't cram your gems too close together or you'll run out of them really quickly. Keep them spaced nice and even for a professional look. Once you get the hang of it, add more dots of glue at a time so the process will go faster.

Other Ideas

* You can add gems to anything, like small mint tins, a cell phone, the straps on a set of shoes, sunglasses, a gift box, a picture frame, and more.

* Instead of using gems that are all the same color, buy different colors and mix them up.

* If you win the lottery and want a real movie star look, buy authentic (and very expensive) Austrian Swarovski crystals for your project. Just thought I'd mention it.

3. Repeat with another gem, placing it about ¼ inch away from the first one—that way the base color of the phone will show through. Keep adding more gems in a row, following the shape of the phone. Finish the first row.

4. Do the second row the same as the first, except now place each gem *between* the two gems above it. Keep adding rows of gems until the front side is covered. Set aside to dry.

5. Now get the handset. Cover one side with gems, just as you did for the base. Let dry.

6. Repeat for the other side of the base and handset. Let dry.

7. Attach the cords, plug in, and start yakking away.

TIP

Don't use any old glue for this project. You want your gorgeous phone to last forever! If you can't use "The Ultimate," go with E6000 glue.

Duct Tape Roses

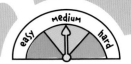

These flirty florals are even better than real flowers because they last forever and are made from something you can find in the garage or supply closet—duct tape! Duct tape comes in a rainbow of colors, which means the options are endless. You can make them into pins, attach them to a hair tie, or sew them onto a handbag.

STUFF YOU'LL NEED

roll of red duct tape
roll of green duct tape
floral wire stem (optional)

How to Do It

1. Tear off a strip of red duct tape about 3 inches long. With the sticky side up, fold the left corner over, as shown.

2. Now fold the right corner down over the left. You should end up with a pointy piece of tape that looks like an arrow.

3. Roll your pointy piece of tape around so it sticks to itself. This is the center of your rose.

TIP You can use scissors to cut the tape, but it will eventually ruin the blade because of the gooey adhesive. Better to just rip it with your fingers.

4. Tear off more strips of red tape. Repeat steps 1 and 2 to make more pointy pieces. One by one, stick them around the center piece, building out until it starts to look like a flower. Make it as big or little as you like.

5. When you're done, make four more pointy pieces using the green tape. Stick them around the flower for leaves.

6. If you want a stem, take a piece of floral wire and hold it up to the bottom of the rose. Tear off a long piece of green tape and wrap it around the bottom of the rose and the top of the floral wire to hold them together. Continue wrapping the green tape around the wire all the way down until it is covered. If you want to add leaves, make more green pointy pieces and stick them onto the stem.

TIP It's okay if your petals aren't all exactly the same size—it will make the rose look more natural.

Other Ideas

* Make a pin out of the roses by poking a small safety pin through the bottom.

* Make a hair clip by using tape to wrap it around the top of a barrette.

* Make smaller roses and string them together on fishing line to make a garland.

* Use one to decorate the top of a gift box.

* Use different colors in the same rose for a bright effect.

TURN UP THE VOLUME!

Here are more ideas for turning up the volume on your accessories.

* Top off an already cute outfit by wearing a silky scarf, either around your head, around your neck, or around your waist.

* Wear a hat! Beanies, floppy brims, and even straw hats add positive posture power!

* Wear sunglasses—but you know that already. Did you ever think about livening up a boring pair by gluing on small crystals or painting on tiny polka dots?

* Check out the secondhand store for a fun vintage purse, then glue on your favorite picture or slap on a cool sticker.

* Use fabric glue to add trim to some ho-hum shorts or pants.

Nature Nut

GARDEN INSPIRATION BRICKS

Next time you are in a sugar-induced reality TV slump, get your booty off the couch and walk outside. Smell the flowers, run your fingers through the soft grass, and listen to the birds chirping. Nature has a lot to offer when it comes to recharging your batteries. Bonding with things like butterflies, ladybugs, and sunflowers soothes the soul in a way that no television show or CD can. So take some time to enjoy the great outdoors and then make yourself some garden-happy gifts. Walking on sunshine—it does a body good.

BUTTON BIRDHOUSE

"NAME THAT PLANT" POKES

BEAUTIFUL BUGS STASH CAN

Beautiful Bugs Stash Can

When was the last time you rolled around on the grass? If you can't remember, start your garden-girl transformation by bringing the outside in. Your room is too small to plant a row of sunflowers and the family just doesn't appreciate a decent bug collection. Think alternative, out of the box. In other words, go for the plastic stuff. You'll simply adore this little gardener's delight stash can. It can hold packs of seeds, lip balm, gardening gloves, tissues, even notes from a secret admirer. A little Astroturf, some rubber bugs, silk flowers—this might even work out for the better because there's nothing to water!

STUFF YOU'LL NEED

- can with removable plastic lid (like a peanut or coffee can)
- piece of Astroturf, 6 x 12 inches (found at any home improvement store)
- assorted rubber bugs like ladybugs, butterflies, houseflies, or beetles
- assorted silk flowers with leaves
- Crafter's Pick "The Ultimate" craft glue
- marker
- rubber bands
- scissors, preferably new

How to Do It

1. Make sure the can is empty, clean, and dry.

2. Lay the Astroturf face down. Set the can on its side with the top lined up against the top edge of the Astroturf. Using the marker, make a line on the Astroturf where the can ends. Cut just under that line to leave room for the lid.

3. Roll the Astroturf around the can until the ends meet, and cut off the extra.

4. Apply a good amount of glue all over the can and on the back of the Astroturf. Let it set a couple minutes to get stiff and gooey. Wrap the Astroturf around the can and attach the rubber bands to hold it in place. Let dry for several hours.

5. Remove the rubber bands. Take a bit of time to arrange the bugs and flowers on the Astroturf. When you like the way they look, glue them in place. Let dry.

TIP If you don't want to mess with the long glue time, use extra-strength double-stick tape instead.

6. Use the glue to add leaves and flowers to the plastic lid.

Other Ideas

* Instead of Astroturf, use green moss, velvet, or construction paper.

* If you don't like bugs, glue flowers all over the can.

* Make a few cans to keep around the house: one for your room, one for the bathroom, and one for the backyard.

FLOWER YOUR FASHION

So you're not into the whole "bonding with the earth" kind of thing? That's fine. But how about adding some fantasy florals to your look? Courtney Scantlin, of San Dimas, California, does just that. She sells her line of sparkly rhinestone-accented flowers to movie stars and fashion models through her company, Girl's Night Out Accessories. Here are her tips for adding flower power to your look.

* Flowers are red-hot accessories right now. Peek into trendy stores to see the latest designs. Then do some brainstorming to create your own versions.

* Wear fake flowers in your hair or attach them to a dress, hat, purse, sandals, even a simple T-shirt.

* Instead of fake flowers, use fresh flowers in your hair or on your clothes for a special event.

* Dry out fresh flowers and then make greeting cards or use them in scrapbooking.

* Put a couple flowers in a bud vase and keep them nearby. It will brighten up both your room and your mood!

TIPS FROM THE EXPERT

79

"Name That Plant" Pokes

easy medium hard

STUFF YOU'LL NEED

Popsicle stick

blank index card, cut in half

decorative paper

clear packing tape

letter stickers or a marker

plant tag with info (these come stuck in the plants when you buy them)

self-laminating sheet

scissors

Choosing plants to buy and take home is the easy part. The hard part is remembering their official names and how to care for them. Whether you are pruning a tree or poking a prickly pear with your finger, it's good to know the 411 on your new leafy amigos.

How to Do It

1. Look at your plant and think of a fun name that fits it, like "Lucille" or "Pinky." Use the letter stickers or markers to put that name on one half of the index card. On the other half, write out the official name of the plant from the plant tag. You can also write down how to care for the plant (such as "keep in bright sunlight"). Wrap two pieces of tape around your finger (sticky side out) and place one on the back of each card.

2. Stick the cards onto a piece of pretty paper. Cut around the cards, leaving a border of the paper.

● full sun
● water

lucille

3. Tape one end of a Popsicle stick to the back of one of the cards. Most of the stick should hang below the card. Now get the other card and lay it on top, right side out. The Popsicle stick should be in the middle. This is your new plant poke.

4. Open the self-laminating sheet and place the plant poke inside. Most of the Popsicle stick should hang out the bottom of the sheet (you don't want to laminate the stick). Close the sheet and smooth it with your fingers so there are no air bubbles. Trim around the edges.

TIP If you don't have a self-laminating sheet, just cover the cards with clear packing tape, or even clear shelf liner.

5. Stick your plant poke in the plant's soil. Now you can walk by your plant and say, "Sweet birdseed from above! Lucille needs water!"

Other Ideas

* Use pretty papers with garden themes to tie the whole look together.

HOW TO MAKE YOUR GARDEN GROW

If the thought of planting a huge garden in your backyard gives you the willies, take baby steps. Try a container garden first. This is a mini flowerbed where you can plant a sampling of small flowers and learn how to take care of them. Here's how to do it.

* Decide where you want to put your garden. Find out how much sun that part of the yard or porch gets. Or is it entirely in the shade?

* Go to your local nursery (a store that grows and sells plants and flowers). Ask someone to help you choose flowers that will do well in the amount of sun or shade your spot gets. You should also pick up potting soil and a rectangular terracotta container (make sure it has drainage holes on the bottom).

* For a cheery look, paint the outside of the container in your favorite colors before you plant the flowers.

* To transfer the plants, pour some of the potting soil into your container. Pat it down gently. Carefully shake each flower out of its holder, keeping the dirt around its roots, and place onto your soil. Pour in more soil and gently pat the soil around the roots.

* Take a gardening class to learn more skills.

* Don't forget to water your garden!

Garden Inspiration Bricks

So you've bought the seeds, picked the corner of the yard, and are all ready to plant your garden and watch it grow. Did you ever think about decorations? We know that things like velvet or, say, glitter won't do well under the open sky, but how about these chunky collage bricks? Your garden will have so much personality that your plants and flowers will emerge from the earth happy and healthy.

STUFF YOU'LL NEED

bricks
mosaic grout (premixed)
Popsicle stick
small items like letter beads, charms, glass pebbles, and mosaic pieces
E6000 glue
craft acrylic paints and paintbrushes (optional)

How to Do It

1. Open the grout and scoop out a hefty glob. Put it on top of the brick and use the Popsicle stick to spread it around like icing. Be sure to cover the entire top.

2. Take your little items and squish them into the grout. Start with the letter beads to make sure you have room to spell out the words or phrases you want. Then add other items all around. Press them firmly in place. Let dry overnight.

3. After the grout is completely dry, try to carefully pull up the items you pressed in. If any come off, add a tiny dab of E6000 glue to the bottom and set them back in place. Let dry.

Other Ideas

* Spell out a poem by putting a phrase on each brick and then arranging the bricks so you can read the whole poem.

* Make your bricks more vibrant by covering the sides with craft acrylic paints. When you're done, seal with a brush-on varnish.

Button Birdhouse

easy | medium | hard

Everyone needs a groovy place to hang out, even our little feathered friends. Help your backyard birds have the coolest pad in the yard with this botanical button birdhouse. It's quite loud, a little funky, and a lot of fun—just like the chirpy chimes you hear coming from the trees at six o'clock in the morning!

STUFF YOU'LL NEED

wooden birdhouse

buttons in assorted sizes

beaded trim

blue painter's tape

fake bird

Crafter's Pick "The Ultimate" craft glue

How to Do It

1. Lay the birdhouse on its side. Pick up one button and squeeze a drop of glue on the back. Set it in place on the birdhouse. You can work in rows or just place the buttons in random fashion. Once that side is covered, let dry for 30 minutes.

2. Turn the birdhouse so another side is facing up. Cover that side in buttons. Continue until the entire birdhouse is covered.

3. Add a line of glue along the edges of the roof and attach the beaded trim. Use little pieces of painter's tape (or masking tape) to hold the trim in place until it dries. Do the same to add trim around the bottom of the birdhouse.

4. Add a thick drop of glue to the bottom of the fake bird and set it at the top of the birdhouse. Let dry.

Other Ideas

❋ Decorate birdhouses in different shapes and sizes, then set them all in a row for a whole bird village.

❋ Instead of buttons, cover your birdhouse in small rocks or mosaic stones.

TIP

Keep a close eye on the buttons as they're drying to make sure they don't slide around. You can add blue painter's tape to hold them in place if needed.

Find

Your Flava

DECORATED DISH SET

Just because you can name—and have tried—every pizza topping and cereal on the planet does not make you the ultimate food expert. Give up the usual routine and go for some gourmet gusto! The yummy ideas in this chapter will show you how to add spice to your supper and flava to your flavor. With a little encouragement, your taste buds will be more adventurous than a mathlete in a mosh pit. By the way, can you pass the fudge sauce?

YUMMY CHOCOLATE BOWLS

CUP O' CANDY

Decorated Dish Set

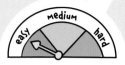

STUFF YOU'LL NEED

plates and/or bowls
rubbing alcohol
cotton balls
Delta Air-Dry Perm Enamel
   Paint in assorted colors
paintbrushes

Imagine what it would be like to get paid to try new foods. It really happens. It's called being a food critic. You go into a restaurant, order an appetizer, main course, and dessert, eat them all, and take notes on what was delish and what was dry as dirt. You then write up a restaurant review, it gets printed, and you move on to the next place. Doesn't that sound like a blast? If you agree, practice the job. Use this exclusive painted plate to taste all the meals that are served in your house. But don't be *too* tough on the in-house chef—you do want to be able to eat breakfast in the morning, you know.

How to Do It

1. Wash and dry the dishes. Put some rubbing alcohol on a cotton ball and rub it all over the outside of the dishes where you are going to paint.

2. Decide what kind of pattern you want (stripes, polka dots, squiggles, whatever). Then go for it! Start with one color of paint and make your designs. Let dry. Move on to the next color, and so on. Don't paint any parts of the dishes that might touch food.

3. When you are done, let the dishes "cure" for six days before you use them. After that, they can be gently hand-washed.

Other Ideas

* Paint coffee mugs as holiday gifts. Put a bag of hot cocoa inside and wrap in clear cellophane.

* Decorate a set of dessert plates.

* Try painting other items, like a big cookie jar, a serving tray, salt and pepper shakers, or a cream and sugar set.

* Decorate a small bowl, then put potpourri in it to make a room freshener.

FUNKIFY YOUR FOOD!

Here are some crazy ways to make your taste buds tingle. Some you will love, others you will hate, but the process of trying new flavors will be a memorable one. Now get brave and go for it!

* Add chocolate chips to microwave popcorn while it's still hot.

* Squeeze lime juice onto your corn on the cob.

* Dip a potato chip in soda pop and eat it really fast.

* Put a drop of chili sauce in your soup.

* Add honey and a little orange juice to berries. Let it all sit for a few minutes, then put it on your yogurt, ice cream, cereal, or in your smoothie.

* Mash up some bananas and put them in your oatmeal.

* Dip corn chips in cottage cheese.

* Eat pickles dipped in peanut butter.

* Add a little hot sauce to your ketchup for a kick!

* Try french fries dipped in a milkshake.

* Put yogurt in your cereal instead of milk.

* Spread cream cheese on your turkey sandwich.

* Dip a potato chip in chocolate sauce.

* Add a slice of pineapple to your hamburger.

* Sprinkle your french fries with pepper.

Yummy Chocolate Bowls

easy medium hard

There's only one thing more mouth-watering than a scoop of your favorite ice cream: your favorite ice cream in a bowl made of chocolate! That's right! Did you ever imagine such a glorious thought? It tastes absolutely heavenly and looks classier than Hilary Duff's prom dress.

STUFF YOU'LL NEED

bag of semi-sweet chocolate chips (or melting chocolates from the craft store)

package of foil baking cups (the kind used for cupcakes)

microwave-safe bowl

wooden spoon

How to Do It

1. Pour the chocolate chips into the bowl. Microwave on high for 30 seconds. Remove and stir. Put the bowl back in for 30 seconds, then stir again. Repeat until the chips are melted into a sauce.

2. Hold a baking cup in your hand. Scoop up some melted chocolate and put it in the cup. Smooth it all around the sides and the bottom. Do the same for five more cups. Put them in the freezer for 10 minutes.

3. Remove the cups from the freezer and add another layer of chocolate. Don't worry if the frozen chocolate gets a bit soft when you spread on the new chocolate. Put the cups back in the freezer for 15 minutes until fully hardened.

4. Remove the cups from the freezer. Make sure your hands are clean, then peel off the foil cups. Be careful to get all the little pieces so you won't eat them!

5. Fill the cups with your favorite dessert. If saving for later, store in a sealed container in the fridge.

Other Ideas

* Use all white chocolate, or use it on just the second layer for a two-tone look.

* Sprinkle chopped nuts or colored sprinkles on the second layer before freezing.

* Fill with ice cream, pudding, fresh fruit, or yogurt.

Cup o' Candy

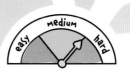

Show someone you care with a cup of sugar. Literally. This candy tree makes a great gift for a teacher, friend, or your Aunt Sally. It's clever, too— after the candies are long gone, the mug is ready for some lip-smacking soup or hot chocolate.

Jolly Rancher courtesy of Hershey Foods, www.jollyrancher.com

STUFF YOU'LL NEED

large mug

stickers (optional)

Styrofoam ball, 4 inches in diameter

bag of wrapped candies (the wrappers must have edges)

box of straight pins

How to Do It

1. If you want, decorate the mug with stickers.

2. Set the Styrofoam ball in the mug. Attach a piece of candy to the ball by poking a pin through the wrapper's edge and pressing it into the foam. Be extra careful with the pins so you don't get poked.

3. Continue adding candies all the way around the bottom of the ball until one row is done.

4. Do the same thing for the second row. Keep going until the entire ball is covered.

5. Set it out to enjoy!

Other Ideas

✿ Use candy with pretty metallic wrappers for a holiday look.

✿ You can use any kind of candy, as long as it has an edge to poke the pin through. There are lots to choose from!

✿ Instead of a mug, use a painted flowerpot or large candleholder.

✿ Ditch the container and use a foam wreath or topiary to hold the candies.

TIP

You'll notice the ball will wobble to one side as you add the candies, but eventually it will stay still after all the candies are on.

89

Glam

GLITTERY WRAPPING PAPER

Do you feel embarrassed when you're at a party and the birthday girl picks up your present to open? Is yours the one with the boring wrapping paper and a lonely little ribbon? If so, it's time to change that a.s.a.p. Yes, picking the right gift is important, but let's face it, a gift that looks good is more fun to give! Gifting with glam is all in the details. Here are three ideas to make sure your presents rock the party.

POWER POP CARDS

AWESOME APPLIQUÉ

Glittery Wrapping Paper

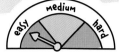

Store-bought paper comes in some far-out styles and patterns. It also comes with a hefty price tag. Think smart and save your money for the gift inside. Pick up a roll of brown packaging paper and go crazy with your favorite foam stamps and micro-glitter. It will make your present shimmer from across the room.

STUFF YOU'LL NEED

- roll of brown packaging paper (found in office supply stores)
- large foam stamps
- craft acrylic paints in assorted colors
- micro-glitter in assorted colors
- blue painter's tape
- scissors

How to Do It

1. Cut off a long piece of the paper. Use painter's tape to secure each corner to the table.

2. Dip your stamp in the paint and press it firmly onto the paper. Quickly pour glitter over the wet paint. Only pour on a little glitter—just enough to cover the paint. Repeat the process, using different stamps and glitters. Let dry.

3. Carefully lift the paper. Bend it gently in half and tap to remove the extra glitter. Roll it up so it won't get creased until it's time to wrap your gift.

Other Ideas

❀ Instead of stamps, draw freehand designs or copy the clip art from pages 140–141.

❀ Use stencils, stickers, or glue-on pictures.

❀ Use this idea to decorate gift bags, too.

TIP You can also use the inside of a brown paper bag as your paper.

Awesome Appliqués

Cure the boring gift-bag blues with some out-of-this-world, awesome appliqués. If you can paint solid colors, cut, and glue, you can totally be a pro at this project.

STUFF YOU'LL NEED

watercolor paper

decorative paper (optional)

foam board, cut into dime-size squares

gems, micro beads, metallic markers (optional)

craft acrylic paints and paintbrushes

white glue

craft glue

scissors

water-based varnish and foam brush (optional)

How to Do It

1. Get the watercolor paper and cut out small, medium, and large versions of shapes like hearts, flowers, and clouds. Paint the shapes and let dry. If you want, outline the edges with another color, or use fancy papers to add borders around the shapes.

2. Take one of the smaller shapes. Use white glue to put two small pieces of foam board on the back, then glue it onto a larger shape. The smaller shape should "pop out" from the larger one. Repeat for the other shapes. These are your appliqués!

3. Decorate the appliqués with metallic pens, gems, and/or beads. For a really polished look, brush on a coat of water-based varnish and let dry.

4. Take each appliqué and glue two more pieces of foam board onto the back. Use craft glue to attach each to the gift bag.

Other Ideas

❋ Copy family pictures and use them to decorate the appliqués.

❋ Cover the shapes with cut-out pics or words from magazines.

❋ Use one of the shapes as a matching gift card.

TIP Don't try to use another kind of paper. Watercolor paper is very thick and bendable, so it will work the best.

Power Pop Cards

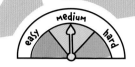

There's nothing too exciting about opening a card—well, unless there's a $100 bill in there. Otherwise, it's the same old "Happy Birthday" message. Or so you thought! Now you can make people gasp in glee with these cooler-than-coolio pop-up cards. Here's how.

STUFF YOU'LL NEED

blank greeting card
assorted decorative papers
bright, bold pictures, photos,
   or stickers to pop up
ruler
glue stick
scissors

How to Do It

1. Cut a strip of paper measuring 1½ inches across. Place it inside the card. Snip off any extra paper that hangs over the edges.

2. Remove the strip from the card. Fold it three times, like an accordion.

3. Apply the glue stick to the strip's outer flaps. Then hold it by the center and place it in the card's fold. Press the two flaps down on both sides of the fold. Use your finger to seal them down. This is the base for your pop-up.

4. Get the picture that you want to pop up. Run the glue stick on the back, along the bottom, and press it onto the base. If you are using a sticker, press the sticker onto a piece of paper and then glue the paper onto the base. Let dry.

5. Decorate the card with drawings, stamps, stickers, sequins, glitter—whatever you want. Now you're poppin'!

BE A GREAT GIFTER

Imagine being a professional shopper! It's all in a day's work for Jaimee Rose of Phoenix, Arizona. She's a newspaper columnist who writes about fashion, shopping, home décor, and more. Jaimee makes gift giving an art because it's her favorite hobby of all time. Here's her advice on the world of presenting presents.

Wrap 'em up

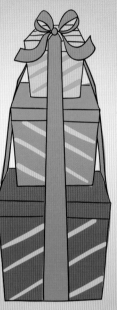

❀ You know how you're always excited to open the biggest, shiniest present first? Put a little extra time into your wrapping and people will adore your gifts before they even see what's inside. Don't be afraid to wrap a special tiny present—like earrings for your mom—in a gigantic box with a big satin bow. Her surprise at discovering the smaller box inside will be part of the fun.

❀ Plain gift wrap is best because you can decorate it with unexpected things, like a pinecone glued on at Christmas.

❀ The inside of a brown paper grocery bag makes perfect wrapping paper. Tie shipping twine in a bow around it and tuck a fresh flower behind the bow. It will look organic and beautiful.

❀ Use real fabric ribbon—that curling stuff gets boring, don't you think? Save ribbons from gifts you've received and reuse them later.

❀ Don't forget tags! Scour your local scrapbook store for pretty ones, like those metal-rimmed tags.

❀ When the December holidays hit, set up a wrapping station in your room and charge your family $2 per package to do the wrapping for them. Let each family member pick a color scheme for their gifts to make them feel like part of the wrapping fun.

❀ Don't wait for holidays to put your wrapping skills to work. Any time you get something special for someone, find a clever way of packaging it. It will be great practice!

Giving and getting

❀ When you give a gift, don't say something like, "If you don't like it, you can take it back." Instead, send out good vibes. Say, "I had so much fun picking this out for you!" while the gift is being unwrapped.

❀ When you receive a gift, of course you have to say thank-you. But also say *why* you love the present. If your sister gives you the new Raven Simone album, maybe you can tell her that you love it because it reminds you of your sister-to-sister dance sessions, jamming to Raven until midnight!

❀ Be careful with "re-gifting"—taking a gift you received and giving it to someone else. Make sure you won't hurt anyone's feelings. This usually means keeping it a very good secret! If your friend gave you a T-shirt for your birthday and you pass it on at the next party, everyone will be upset. But if you get lip gloss at a school holiday party that isn't your color and pass it to your cousin who lives in another state, that's an okay trade.

Spirit

School, homework, chores, taking care of Noodles, the family iguana—life can sure stress a little lady out. When you don't release that bottled-up energy, it can make you cranky and uptight. That is so not your true style. You are all about sending positive vibes, right? So go get comfy and see what wonderful revelations lie before you when you take the time to soothe your inner spirit.

SCORPIO'S
BATH SALTS
TAKE TIME TO
SMELL THE
ROSES

VEG-OUT MEDITATION PILLOW

EXOTIC TRAVELS DREAM BOOK

DREAMS

TRAVEL

Horoscope Bath Salts

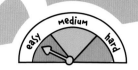

GEMINI'S
BATH SALTS
PEP-UP PEPPERMINT
TO GET YOU ON
YOUR FEET!

CAPRICORN'S
BATH SALTS
LOVELY LAVENDER
TO CALM YOU
DOWN, GIRL!

SCORPIO'S
BATH SALTS
TAKE TIME TO
SMELL THE
ROSES

Does your Capricorn friend need to chill out? Does your Gemini girl need to stop giggling at everything in sight? Help her take it down a notch by mixing up a batch of horoscope bath salts fine-tuned to her personality. Then send her home for a relaxing soak in the tub. It might be a good idea for you, too!

STUFF YOU'LL NEED

½ cup rock salt (found at gourmet grocery stores)

3 tablespoons Epsom salts

1 tablespoon baking soda

food coloring

plastic baggie with press-and-seal closure

essential oils (see page 99 to choose your oil)

food coloring

5-ounce glass jar

metal-rimmed tag

decorative paper

hole punch

white string

glue stick

scissors

How to Do It

1. Open a plastic baggie and put in the rock salt, Epsom salts, and baking soda. Add 2–3 drops of food coloring. Seal the bag and squish it around with your fingers so everything gets all smashed together.

2. Open the bag and add 2–3 drops of essential oil to scent your mixture. Close the bag again and squish, squish, squish some more.

3. Carefully pour your mixture into the jar. Use a skinny spoon or a plastic funnel if that makes it easier.

4. Make a label to hang from the jar telling what it is and how to use it. Write or print out the info on a piece of pretty paper. Make sure to keep it small enough so it will fit on the label tag. Use a glue stick to attach the paper to the tag. Repeat for the other side. Punch a hole at the top of the label. Thread the string through and tie it to the jar.

PICKING YOUR OIL

Find your (or your friend's) sign, then use that oil for the bath salts. Essential oils are easy to find in health food stores, craft stores, and some grocery stores.

If your birthday is...	your sign is...	and your oils are...
January 20–February 18	AQUARIUS	lavender or patchouli
February 19–March 20	PISCES	sandalwood or ylang-ylang
March 21–April 19	ARIES	frankincense or ginger
April 20–May 20	TAURUS	oakmoss or ylang-ylang
May 21–June 20	GEMINI	lavender or peppermint
June 21–July 22	CANCER	chamomile or palmarosa
July 23–August 22	LEO	sweet orange or lime
August 23–September 22	VIRGO	patchouli or oakmoss
September 23–October 22	LIBRA	rose or ylang-ylang
October 23–November 21	SCORPIO	pine or cardamom
November 22–December 21	SAGITTARIUS	rosemary or clove
December 22–January 19	CAPRICORN	cypress or patchouli

TIP For more information on horoscopes, checkout www.astrology.com.

SALT SENSE

Instead of making bath salts to match your sign, whip up a batch to suit your or your friend's mood. Here's how.

If you want to...	use this oil...
CHEER UP	jasmine or ylang-ylang
IMPROVE YOUR MEMORY	rosemary or peppermint
BE MORE ENERGETIC	grapefruit, ginger, or lemon
SLEEP BETTER	lavender and vanilla mixed together, or chamomile
BE MORE SELF-CONFIDENT	bay laurel, cypress, rosemary, or orange
GET RID OF ANGER	neroli, patchouli, rose, or chamomile
BE LESS STRESSED-OUT	rose, patchouli, lavender, mandarin, or sandalwood

Exotic Travels Dream Book

Globetrotting around the world sounds dreamy, doesn't it? But if that passport is still a ways away, indulge your fantasies in your very own room. Excited about Egypt? Longing for London? Use this book as a place for souvenirs of your travels, or as a book of wishes for places you'd still like to see.

STUFF YOU'LL NEED

cardboard baby book (found at the dollar store or bookstore)

decorative paper

pictures

letter stickers, pens, and markers

glitter, rubber stamps, and other things to decorate with

glue stick

white glue

scissors

TIP When you go on a trip, pick up little souvenirs like tickets, brochures, sugar packets, and tokens, and use them on your pages.

How to Do It

1. Think of a theme for your book—do you want it to be about one place, or a whole bunch of places? Go online or visit travel offices to get pictures and info about the place or places you chose.

2. Open the book to the first page. Spread white glue all over the page, from edge to edge. (Don't use too much glue or it will ruin your paper.) Lay the decorative paper on the page and smooth with your fingers. Trim off any extra.

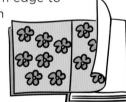

3. Glue a picture onto the page. Add other elements all around the page. It's okay to overlap pictures—that makes it more interesting. Leave spaces to write notes, phrases, or thoughts about why you want to see the place, or happy memories of your last vacation.

4. Continue for the other pages.

YOGA 101

Ooooummmm. Breathe in deeply. Now let it out. Feel better? That's the energy of yoga. Adrienne J. Li Causi, a yoga instructor in Phoenix, Arizona, took time away from her class to teach us the basics.

❀ **So what is yoga, anyway?** Yoga is a practice developed in India many, many years ago. It combines movement with breathing and meditation. Yoga helps us discover our true selves.

❀ **How do I do it?** Start by putting on loose, comfortable clothes. Find a quiet place where you can sit comfortably.

Close your eyes and focus on your breathing. Try not to think about anything except your breath moving in and out. There may be a thought that comes into your mind—this is natural, but when it happens just start thinking about your breathing again. Try to do this for 3–5 minutes. Eventually you will be able to sit for longer periods of time.

Once you're relaxed, try doing the poses in the order given here. Each one should flow into the next, with your body going naturally through the movements. This is great because it releases tension, brings you inner peace, and makes you feel good inside and out! When you're finished, keep relaxing with a cup of hot herbal tea and a good book.

❀ **Downward dog** Start by getting down on all fours. Tuck your toes under, lift up your knees, and act like a dog that is stretching its bottom. Take a few deep breaths.

❀ **Upward dog** Lay down on your belly. Put your hands flat on the floor beside your chest. Push the ground away from you and lift your upper body off the floor. Look up and take your hips off the ground, too. Breathe!

❀ **Cat** Come back to all fours. Arch your spine up to the sky, like a cat. Breathe out.

❀ **Cow** Breathe in as you drop your belly toward the ground and look up.

❀ **Forward bend** Now stand up. Bend your knees slightly. Slowly bend forward and reach your hands toward the ground. Take some deep breaths.

❀ **Mountain** Stand straight up again. Lift your head as though there was a magic pillow resting behind it.

TIPS FROM THE EXPERT

101

Veg-out Meditation Pillow

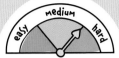

STUFF YOU'LL NEED

4 different types of silky, shiny fabric, ¼ yard each

batting

sewing machine or needle and thread

2 packages of pretty trim

straight pins

scissors

Every chica needs time to chillax. What better way to do that than to plop down on this silky smooth mediation pillow made for *you* by *you*? Create a little area in your room where you can set it on the floor. Whenever you need to calm down, you'll have a special spot ready and waiting for you.

How to Do It

1. Fold each piece of fabric down the middle (widthwise) and cut along the fold, so you get two small pieces of each kind. You should end up with 8 pieces of fabric.

2. Separate the fabric into two sets. Each set should have the same 4 pieces.

If you don't feel like going to the fabric store, cut up old T-shirts (ask permission first) and use them instead.

3. Take the first set. Lay two of the pieces together, right side in. Pin along the short edge. Sew along the edge and then remove the pins. Now repeat for the other two pieces. You should end up with two long pieces of fabric.

4. Now you will sew these two long pieces together. Lay them together, right side in. Pin along one of the long sides. Sew and remove the pins.

5. Repeat steps 3 and 4 for the second set of fabric. You will now have the front and back panels of your pillow.

6. Lay the panels together, right side in. Pin along the two long sides and one short side. Sew in place and remove the pins. One short end should still be open.

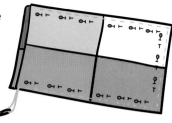

7. Turn the pillow sleeve inside out. Unroll the batting and open it. Fold it in a layered, rectangular fashion, so it will fit to the shape of your pillow. Stuff it inside the sleeve. Fold over the raw, open edges to make a clean-looking hem and pin. Sew shut.

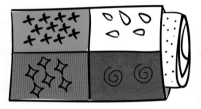

8. Pin the trim onto both ends of the pillow, then sew in place.

9. Fluff the pillow so it looks nice and even. Mmmmmm, doesn't your mind feel clearer already?

Other Ideas

* Use bigger or smaller pieces of fabric to make different size pillows.

* If you don't want four types of fabric, just stick with one kind to make it easier.

* Instead of putting your pillow on the floor, put it on your bed for a luxurious look.

TIP

Take your time with this project. Double-check before you cut, and make sure you have the fabric lined up correctly before you sew.

Locker

Lockers can be your best friend or your worst nightmare. It's all in the organizing, ya know? Whether you're an extreme neat freak or a toss-'n'-go kind of student, the least you can do is decorate those cold, bare metal walls with stuff that makes you smile. Here's some locker 911 to get you started.

BEADED BOOK COVERS

NIFTY NOTE HOLDERS

Friendly Faces Mirror

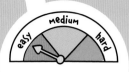

easy medium hard

STUFF YOU'LL NEED

round mirror that will fit inside your locker

yearbook from your school

small glass pebbles (found in craft, plant, or pet stores)

crêpe paper in your school's colors (or any colors)

white glue

Crafter's Pick "The Ultimate" craft glue

extra-strength double-sided adhesive strips

scissors

School isn't school without friends. They're there to give you a hug when you need one, and to set you straight when you are embarrassing yourself in public. It's swell to keep them on your mind, which is a cinch with this friendly faces mirror. You can fix your hair and say "ciao" to your buddies at the same time.

How to Do It

1. Make photocopies or scans of your friends' pictures from the yearbook. Cut them out.

2. Take a glass pebble. Add a drop of white glue to the back and set it over one of the yearbook pictures. Press firmly to squeeze out any extra glue. Let dry until the glue is clear. Repeat with more pebbles until you have enough to go all around the mirror.

3. Lay the mirror face up on a flat surface. Squeeze a line of craft glue all around the edge. Now press the picture pebbles into the glue. Let dry.

4. Flip the mirror over. Squeeze another line of glue around the edge of the back. Cut a long strip of crepe paper. Starting with the end of the

Don't hang the mirror on the door of your locker—keep it on the wall so it won't fall or break every time you slam your locker door shut.

Other Ideas

❋ Don't use pebbles at all—glue the pictures directly onto the mirror.

❋ Use lace or other kinds of trim instead of crepe paper.

strip, press it into the glue so that half of it hangs over the edge of the mirror. Scrunch the crepe paper as you glue it down to give it a finished, ruffled look. Let dry.

5. Add another line of glue on top of the crepe paper. Repeat step 4 with the other color crepe paper so it creates a second border. Let dry.

6. Leave the mirror lying face down. Get the adhesive strips and peel off one side of the protective backing. Stick them all around the mirror's back to make sure it will hold securely to your locker. When you go to hang it, remove the other backings and press it onto the locker wall.

CREATE AN ULTRA-COOL LOCKER LOUNGE

I know, I *know*—your locker feels as tiny as a sardine can. But believe it or not, there are ways to make that squishy space as funky as your bedroom. Here is a list to get you started.

❋ Cover the walls with fake fur, Astroturf, or corkboard.

❋ Pick up some adorable rear-view mirror ornaments from the auto section at the store and tape them to the ceiling of your locker so they hang down.

❋ Make your locker smell fruity fresh by keeping an air freshener or potpourri inside.

❋ Buy a stack of button magnets and store them on the door so you can use the walls as a memo board.

❋ Hang up a small dry-erase board to keep track of your homework assignments.

❋ Keep a set of magnetic poetry in your locker so you can post messages on the door (inside or outside).

❋ Put a little box in the front of your locker for secret notes that come throughout the day.

❋ Buy long fringe at the fabric store and tape it along the inside top of your locker, so when you open the door it hangs in front.

❋ Make your locker a mini-office where all your extra supplies are stored: box of pencils, small stapler, hole punch, small sharpener, markers, perfume, lipstick.

Nifty Note Holders

STUFF YOU'LL NEED

- clothespin (one for each note holder)
- wooden shapes (found at the craft store)
- craft acrylic paints in assorted colors
- paintbrushes
- stickers, gems, squeeze glitter
- markers
- thick button magnet
- Crafter's Pick "The Ultimate" craft glue

Before you can ace your spelling test on Friday, you have to know where that spelling list is. Just yesterday it was under your English book, and this morning you saw it floating on top of your gym clothes. Shave off the stress of searching by making a set of these nifty clips to hold the must-see paperwork of the day. They will make your life *mucho* easier!

TIP Don't decorate your shapes with things that are too heavy or the clips will slide down.

How to Do It

1. Paint the clothespins and wooden shapes. Let dry.

2. Decorate the shapes with phrases such as "Today," "Ta-Da!," and "To Do." Add glitter and gems to make them look super flashy. Let dry.

3. Add a glob of craft glue to the front of each clothespin and attach a shape. Let dry. Flip it over and add a glob of glue to the back. Attach the button magnet. Let dry.

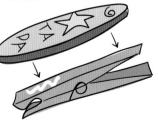

4. Hang them in your locker and use them to post your most important papers!

Other Ideas

❋ Use other words, such as the days of the week or school subjects.

❋ Instead of writing words on the shapes, cut out letters from magazines and paste them on.

❋ Skip the cutouts and glue a big fake flower on the clip, or small, funky toys from the party store.

Beaded Book Covers

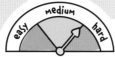

Instead of frowning every time you pull out that 10-pound history textbook, pep it up with this beaded book cover. All it takes is some sequins, beads, thread, and a little bit of time to have the best dang book in class.

STUFF YOU'LL NEED

nylon book cover (found at the craft, book, or discount department store)

sequins

small beads

needle and thread that matches the book cover

scissors

Other Ideas

✿ Instead of beads, use small buttons.

✿ Theme your book covers to match your classes, so your books will be easier to grab out of your locker.

TIP Don't use one long piece of thread to sew on all the beads because when you put the cover on the book, the thread will break and beads will fly everywhere.

How to Do It

1. Cut a piece of thread about 12 inches long and thread the needle. Tie a knot at the end, leaving a 1-inch tail.

2. Poke the needle through the book cover from the inside. Let the needle come halfway through and then slide on a sequin, followed by a bead. Now pull the needle all the way through. Make sure the sequin and bead stay down next to the book cover.

3. Bring the needle over the bead, back through the hole of the sequin, and down through the fabric.

4. Pull the needle tight and snip off the thread, leaving a 1-inch tail. Tie the two tails together in a double knot.

5. Repeat steps 2–4 all over the rest of the book cover.

Your Jewelry

By now you are so over the little-girl plastic jewelry, right? Having a nice jewelry assortment will do wonders for your wardrobe, as well as your mood. So let's clean out the old and bring in the new! Lucky for you, jewelry and crafting go together like hot wings and ranch dressing—they're a winning combination. If you can work a pair of needle-nose pliers and have an eye for color, you can create oodles of one-of-a kind bracelets, earrings, pins, and more. Excited? You will be after you see what's in store!

WORDS-OF-THE-WISE BRACELETS

METAL EDGE NAME NECKLACE

ELEGANT EARRINGS AND NECKLACE

Words-of-the-Wise Bracelets

Express yourself, baby! These witty word bracelets will earn major snaps when you flash your wrist. Make a list of all the crazy words, phrases, or names you hear or say and then slide them on a strand of stretchy string. They are guaranteed to have onlookers *ooo* and *ahhhh*, as well as shout things like, "I HAVE to have this!"

STUFF YOU'LL NEED

roll of Stretch Magic string (found in the craft store)

small beads in assorted colors

letter beads

scissors

How to Do It

1. Make a list of the words you want on your bracelets. Open your bag of letter beads and spread them out on the table. Pull out the letters for your words and set them aside.

2. Cut a piece of string 6 inches long. Tie a knot at one end, leaving a little bit of a tail.

3. Slide on enough colored beads to cover 2-3 inches of string. Now slide on the letter beads to spell your word. If you're using a phrase with more than one word, put a colored bead between words. When you're done, slide on more colored beads.

4. Wrap the bracelet around your wrist to see if you need to make it longer by adding more beads. When you have the right size, tie the two ends together in a double knot. Snip off the extra string.

Other Ideas

❃ Spell out the names of your friends.

❃ Cut the string longer to make ankle bracelets, or shorter to make rings.

❃ To make a double bracelet, tie two beaded strands together.

❃ Use larger letter beads and string them on strips of leather, then tie them to key rings for key chains.

Metal Edge Name Necklace

Introduce your sassy self to the world by wearing your name in living color. The beauty of this project is that you can design it to match your personality and mood. Plus, it's so cheap to make that you can have one for every day of the year!

STUFF YOU'LL NEED

your name printed in a fun font from the computer (any kind of paper will do)

self-laminating sheet

copper or foil tape (found at the craft store)

hole punch

large jump ring

necklace cording (any cord or chain is fine)

scissors

How to Do It

1. Cut your name out of the sheet of paper.

2. Insert the paper in the laminating sheet and seal. Use your fingers to smooth out any air bubbles. Cut around the paper in a rectangle. This is your nameplate.

3. Cut off four pieces of the copper or foil tape. Carefully apply them around the edges of the nameplate.

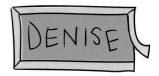

4. Punch a hole at the top, either horizontally or vertically (depending on how you want your name to hang). Open a jump ring and stick it through the hole, then squeeze the jump ring shut. Thread the cording through the jump ring and tie a knot at the ends to secure.

TIP

Make sure the words aren't too big—you don't want to look like a walking billboard! Also, stick with a font that's easy to read so people won't be poking their noses in your neck.

Other Ideas

❀ Instead of your name, print out a word like "spoiled," "crafty," "diva," or "chica."

❀ Use smaller fonts to make smaller words, then use them as charms for a bracelet or key chain.

113

Elegant Earrings and Necklace

Huge door-knocker earrings and heavy chokers not your thang? No worries girl, clean and simple will make just as much of a statement. This recipe is a real winner, not only because you can make multiple sets to match all your killer clothing ensembles, but also because they're a snap to put together.

STUFF YOU'LL NEED

For the earrings:

4 mini seed beads

2 small beads

2 head pins, each 1 inch long

2 fishhook earrings

needle-nose pliers

For the necklace:

assorted beads

thin organza ribbon, ½ yard long

necklace closure

scissors

How to Do It

1. Start with the earrings. Take a head pin and slide on one mini seed bead. Now slide on a small bead, followed by another seed bead.

2. Hold the beads tightly on the head pin and insert it through the hole at the bottom of the fishhook earring. Use the needle-nose pliers to carefully bend the end of the head-pin wire over and pinch it in place so it won't come out. Repeat steps 1 and 2 for the other earring.

TIP

For the necklace, try to find beads that have big openings. If you choose beads for your earrings that are kind of big, use longer head pins.

3. To make the necklace, trim one end of the organza ribbon to a very sharp, pointy angle. Thread the beads onto the ribbon, one by one. Spread them out to look even. They won't slide because the ribbon will "grip" them.

4. Tie one half of the clasp hook to one end of the ribbon and the other half to the opposite end.

Other Ideas

* Use longer head pins to make longer earrings.

* Make your own beads with oven-bake clay.

* Use the same method to make bracelets or anklets.

THE BUSINESS OF BAUBLES

High school algebra homework? Doing the family dishes after dinner? Designing, making, and selling a line of semi-precious stone jewelry? It's a no-sweat combo for 13-year-old Cassy Saba of Chandler, Arizona. She got started when she was only 10 years old and she made a piece for her mom. Her mom wore it to work and came home with a list of orders. These days, Cassy's jewelry sells at high-end boutiques for about $100 a piece. Here are her tips for getting your own line of jewelry started.

* Start small. Having a jewelry business is a really big task that takes up a lot of your personal time. It takes a while for a business to get noticed, so work your way up and you will do a great job.

* Start by using inexpensive plastic beads so you can go crazy coming up with lots of designs. Once you've nailed down your designs, work your way up to more pricey beads.

* Look through magazines to find ideas. Grab a sketchpad and draw out your visions.

* Try to think of fun, trendy things that haven't been done before.

* Have fun mixing and matching colors and textures.

* Think big! As you make your pieces, imagine seeing them in fashion magazines or on movie stars. It's great motivation!

* Have your mom or dad help you with the business angle. Whatever money you collect, use at least part of it to buy more supplies for your next sale!

Tune In

Music makes the world go round, but it isn't just about toting your CD player around 24/7 and playing your favorite tunes. There are plenty of other ways to show you're geared for groovin'. While you're at it, why not soak up some new artists? It may open the door to new friendships (hint hint, like the cute guy who always wears the Linkin Park T-shirt). Whether it's Ashlee Simpson's onstage boo-boo or the cuteness level of Maroon 5's lead singer, music is the one thing everyone LOVES to dish about. So go put a few discs in the player because the ideas ahead are all about enhancing your personality with some rad, remarkable art that you can make and share.

CONCERT COLLAGE STOOL

RETRO RECORD ALBUM SCRAPBOOK

"It's a Hit" Photo Frames

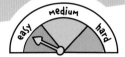

Music collectors go goo-goo over the simplest of finds. But you don't have to be a pro to know that these 45 records from days gone by make super-cool wall decorations. This will be the fastest, easiest project ever, and it will be the one that gets the most "Oh, how neat!" comments.

How to Do It

1. Choose records with funny song titles that fit with the people or pictures you're framing. Place the picture behind the record, making sure the person's face shows through the hole. Remove it. Lay the record face down and rub the glue stick on the back of the label around the hole. Line up the picture and press into the glue. Let dry.

2. Turn the record face up. Use squeeze paint to add dots around the hole and the edge of the record. Write out the place and date if you like. Let dry.

3. Flip the record over again, face down. Use E6000 glue to attach a sawtooth picture hanger. Let dry, then hang!

Other Ideas

❋ Instead of hanging it on the wall, rest the record on a little folding plate stand and display on a tabletop.

❋ Be creative and make your own label for the record. Simply put a piece of paper on top of the record and use a pencil to trace the shape. Cut it out, decorate it, and use the glue stick to stick it on.

❋ Instead of squeeze paint, use tiny gems.

MAKING THE PERFECT MIX

My sister, Theresa Cano, is a self-proclaimed music freak. She owns more than 1,000 CDs and considers making mix CDs part of her daily ritual. That obsession led to a job at an entertainment web site, where she gets to review concerts and such. Here are her tips for making the best mix.

❋ One of the best gifts you can give someone is a mix tape or CD. Choose songs for their personality and combine them in one A-plus compilation.

❋ Pick themes for your mixes, such as "car ride," "chicks who rock," "rainy day," or "divas unite."

❋ The secret is to just throw a bunch of your favorite songs together. Somehow it always sounds good because it's what you love to hear.

❋ If you have access to an online music store, you can burn discs (with mom and dad's permission), otherwise go old school. Put a blank tape in your boom box and wait for your favorite songs to come on the radio so you can record them.

❋ If you have a dual cassette box, you can arrange the songs any way you want. The process is time-consuming, but the hunt is the best part!

TIPS FROM THE EXPERT

119

Retro Record Album Scrapbook

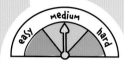

STUFF YOU'LL NEED

record album cover

colored tape (found in the hardware section of grocery stores and discount department stores)

stack of scrapbook paper, each sheet 12 x 12 inches

hole punch

3 binder rings

pencil

scissors

Believe it or not, your parents were once too cool for their own good. They turned the beat around with these weirdo things called "record albums." They probably have some stashed in your very house right now. The album covers not only protected the records inside but also served as pieces of pop art because of their wacky but still divine designs. I doubt mom or dad will let you take a pair of scissors to their stash, but you can always check out the local thrift store for deals. Pick up an album and make this easy scrapbook to hold all of your concert stubs, concert fliers, stickers, and more.

How to Do It

1. Carefully cut apart the record album cover so you have two separate pieces. Apply the colored tape in an even line all around the edges of both pieces. These are the front and back of your scrapbook.

2. Line up both pieces and punch three holes along the edge.

TIP

If the stack of paper is too thick to punch holes through, separate it into smaller stacks and punch through one stack at a time.

Other Ideas

❀ If you want the covers to last for an extra long time, take them to a local copy center and have them laminated first.

❀ Use a glue stick to add a pocket to the inside cover so you can hold things you want to put in the book.

❀ Look for 45-rpm records and make smaller scrapbooks.

❀ If your parents have a favorite band from the past, find one of its albums and make a scrapbook as a gift for them.

3. Lay the stack of scrapbook paper on top of the bottom cover. Now put the front cover back on top. Make sure the bottom cover, paper, and top cover are all neatly lined up along the punched edge.

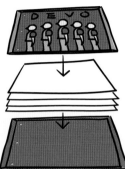

4. Use the pencil to trace around the punched holes onto the paper, so you know where to make the punches. Take out the stack of paper and punch holes through your outlines.

5. Sandwich all the pieces back together. Insert the binder rings through the holes. Snap shut. Add stickers or whatever you like to the cover.

JOINING THE MUSIC BIZ

Do you dream about working in the music business? If so, here are a couple of ideas to get you started on the right track.

❀ If you think you might want to perform, take a class or join your school band. Ask your teacher if you can try all the instruments to see which you like best. Practice, practice, practice, then offer to give shows for your family or neighbors. Don't forget to make a marquee, admission tickets, and freshen up your autograph. This early concert thing is good—it will help you get over stage fright early.

❀ If you're more the type to review music rather than play it, write your own concert or CD review by jotting down in your journal what you saw or heard. Think about what the songs sounded like, what they were about, the best and worst songs, and so on. Most artists have message boards; post your personal reviews there. Also, read reviews online or in music magazines to learn the tricks. Submit your piece to the school newspaper—maybe it will get printed!

Concert Collage Stool

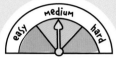

There are only so many stickers that will fit on your notebook, and dad's temples will throb if you slap one on your bedroom door. Think functional. Transform a boring stool from the discount department store into a rocker girl's dream chair. That smooth, flat surface is an empty canvas just waiting to be covered with labels of your favorite bands.

STUFF YOU'LL NEED

stool

craft acrylic paints and paintbrushes

music magazine you don't mind cutting up

assorted stickers and/or pictures of your favorite music stars

water-based varnish and brush

leather fringe trim

sequin trim

white glue

Crafter's Pick "The Ultimate" craft glue

scissors

How to Do It

1. Paint the legs of the stool and let dry. Add painted details if you want. Let dry.

2. Tear out a couple of pages from the magazine. Cut each page into 6–8 pieces. Use white glue to apply them to the seat of the stool. You want to overlap them so the whole seat is covered.

TIP Use a clean paintbrush to apply the glue—it will go on more evenly. If you don't want to cut up your magazines, go to the local copy center and make color copies.

3. Lay out all your pictures and stickers on the seat of the stool. Move them around until you find a look you like. Glue or stick them on. Try to have them facing in all directions so the stool will look good however you look at it.

4. Cover the entire stool with a layer of varnish. Let dry. Apply another coat.

5. Add a line of craft glue around the seat of the stool. Let it set for a few minutes until it is tacky to the touch, then apply the fringe. Let dry. Add a line of glue just above the fringe and attach the sequin trim. Let dry.

Other Ideas

❋ You can make a stool of all your favorite bands, or just of one artist.

❋ Make a matching stool of actors and actresses.

❋ Go to a music store and buy song music sheets, then use those to cover the seat.

❋ To protect the seat even better, cover it with clear vinyl and staple the vinyl underneath.

BUST A MOVE AND TRY NEW TUNES

Rock have you in a rut? Techno got 'cha trippin'? Pop leave you parched? Have no fear! It's never too late to try new cuts and venture into uncharted territory. Even if you don't like everything you hear, you can at least describe the reasons why.

❋ To learn more about different kinds of music, change your radio station for a few minutes each day. Trade CDs with your friends to hear what kind of music they listen to. Ask mom and dad what they like, as well as your other family members. You just may get turned on to some new stuff!

❋ Go to music stores and see what the clerks have chosen for their "pick of the week."

❋ Read about music in *Rolling Stone, Teen People,* and *Spin.*

❋ Visit online music stores like iTunes.com or Amazon.com and listen to sample tracks.

❋ Listen to the soundtracks of movies and TV shows that feature new artists.

❋ Always give a new band a chance. Be open to everything!

Money

DECOUPAGED DOMINOES

At some point, the thought of making some dough off your colorful creations may cross your mind. It's not a crazy goal—there are scores of other hip chicks just like you who are already doing it. Or maybe you have yet to make something, but just want to fatten your piggy bank. Earning your own cash and saving it can lead to awesome things like a new pair of jeans, art supplies, even a fabulous vacation. Count your pennies and spend wisely, and you're on the right track. Peek ahead for some moneymaking ideas to put you on the path to livin' large.

FAUX STAINED GLASS JARS

"IT TAKES MONEY TO MAKE MONEY" CASH BOX

Decoupaged Dominos

STUFF YOU'LL NEED

box of dominos

small pictures or stickers

sequins, micro-glitter, gems, and so on

craft acrylic paints and paintbrushes

3-D squeeze paint

strong button magnets

white glue

water-based varnish and brush

scissors

People love to stick things on their fridge. Don't believe me? Just count the number of kooky items on your family's refrigerator! Next time you're looking to make a few bucks, whip up a batch of these and sell them to friends and family. The bolder and brighter, the better. Suggested sale price: $2 each.

How to Do It

1. Cut out small pictures that will fit on the dominos.

2. Apply a layer of glue on the top (the flat side) of the domino. Lay the picture on top. Smooth out any bubbles with your fingers.

3. Brush a layer of varnish over the domino to seal it. Let dry.

4. Line the edges of the dominos with paint, squeeze paint, and/or micro-glitter. Glue on sequins or tiny gems if desired. Let dry.

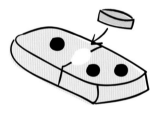

5. Flip the dominos over. Add a drop of glue to the back of each and press on a magnet. Let dry. Store each in a little plastic baggie until sold.

Other Ideas

✿ Use E6000 glue to attach a jump ring on the back of each domino. Let dry, then string a piece of cording through to make a necklace.

NEED SOME DOUGH?

Saving for a big trip, a birthday present for your best friend, or maybe an iPod? Check out this list of ideas for padding your wallet—and then keeping it that way!

Make some money...

❄ Start a Saturday morning dog-walking service for your neighbors.

❄ Ask your grandparents to hire you for a day to do small chores, like watering plants, scooping doggie poop, dusting the furniture, or sorting their DVD collection.

❄ Hold a garage sale and sell your old toys and clothes.

❄ Start a babysitting service in your neighborhood.

❄ Put those piano/singing/tap dancing lessons to good use: perform at family events and put out a tip jar!

❄ Start a wake-up or reminder service for your family and friends. They pay you to give them a wake-up call or to remind them of upcoming events. You can also start an email newsletter with family info that they can subscribe to.

❄ Rent out your video games, DVDs, and books to friends and family. Get a little journal to keep track of who has what.

❄ Start a personalization service. Use your crafty supplies to decorate coffee mugs, sneakers, or tote bags for customers. Offer to put their names on in fancy lettering.

Then save it!

❄ When birthdays and holidays come around, make your gifts and greeting cards instead of buying them.

❄ Open a bank account, or have your grandparents keep your money for you.

❄ Instead of buying new clothes, have a clothing swap with your friends. Everyone brings a few items of clothing they don't want anymore or that don't fit. You put them in the middle of the room and everyone takes a turn choosing something from the pile and trying it on. Everyone leaves with something new!

❄ Keep a money journal to track what you spend your money on. It will help you see your spending patterns!

❄ Always take a little bit out of the money you make and put it away. For example, if you sell a bracelet for five dollars, give yourself $4.50 to spend and put fifty cents in savings. You'll be surprised how quickly it adds up!

❄ Shop at the dollar store for little things like hair clips, lip gloss, even art supplies.

❄ Whenever you go shopping, make a list beforehand so you'll stay focused and won't splurge on extra things you don't need.

Faux Stained Glass Jars

STUFF YOU'LL NEED

baby food jars, washed and with labels removed

self-laminating sheets

Sharpie markers in assorted colors

black permanent fine-point marker

ribbon

white glue

People *looove* to organize. From the silverware drawer to office supplies, there is something soothing about keeping things neat and tidy. Especially when you have neato containers like these for sorting. They look like stained glass, but they're not. Make up a bunch and watch the customers get in line. Suggested sale price: $4 each.

How to Do It

1. Save a label from one of the baby food jars to use as your template. Your self-laminating sheet will have one thick side and one thin side (the thin side has the sticky back). Place the sheet on the table with the thin side up. Lay the baby food label on top and draw around the shape. Make more outlines on the rest of the sheet.

TIP

Tell people they can use the jars to hold coins, buttons, pencils, or any small items that seem to gather as clutter.

2. Get swirly! Use the markers to draw circles and curvy shapes all over the sheet. Don't even think about making perfect designs— the idea is to make it colorful and fun. When the sheet is completely covered, take the black fine-point marker and outline some of the shapes or draw swirls or little stars or polka dots.

3. Cut out the shapes you outlined. Peel off the thick sheet and carefully place the sticky side on the jar. Do this to all the jars. It will look like you decorated right on the glass—very catchy looking!

4. Add a line of glue around the rim of the jar and apply the ribbon. Press in place and let dry.

Other Ideas

* Instead of random shapes, draw different kinds of flowers.

* Instead of the baby food label, use small stencils to make your shapes.

* Cut out bigger shapes and put them on large glass vases or larger jars.

SHOW AND SELL!

Think you have what it takes to put your goods up for sale? I think you do. Here are some notes to help you along the way. Good luck, and don't forget the little people!

* Have your friends test out your items first to find any flaws. Make sure to fine-tune them before even thinking about putting them out for sale.

* Keep track of how much your supplies cost and how much time it took to make your items so you can price them right.

* Always tag everything with your name—it looks more professional.

* Have a yard sale to see how the crowd responds to your work. If all goes well, ask your parents to help you reserve space at a local craft show.

* Make some flyers telling people where they can buy your work.

* Be sure you have enough merchandise made before you put things on sale. You don't want to run out before the show even starts!

* Have a little home party to sell your crafts. Invite everyone on the block.

* Once you are confident in your work, look in the local paper to find small boutiques. Call the owner and ask to make an appointment to show your work.

handcrafted by Kathy

"It Takes Money to Make Money" Cash Box

STUFF YOU'LL NEED

- wooden cigar box
- 2 rolls of pennies
- gold and green craft acrylic paint
- paintbrushes
- jar of premixed grout
- plastic knife
- damp sponge
- paper towels
- large bag of small acrylic gems
- play money (bills)
- 4 1-inch wooden balls that are flat on one side
- Crafter's Pick "The Ultimate" craft glue
- Scrabble letter tiles (optional)

"It takes money to make money" is a popular theme in business. It means that in order to start selling lemonade, you first need money to buy the lemons, cups, and art supplies to make the signs. Don't ever forget that. Actually, you won't be able to forget it because this copper-covered cash box will always be there to remind you. Think of it as your good luck charm. And with all these coins, at least you know you will never be broke!

How to Do It

1. Open the rolls of pennies. Take one and put a dab of glue on the back. Press it in the lower right-hand corner of the lid. Keep gluing on pennies, working in rows until the entire lid is covered. Let dry.

2. Paint the rest of the box green and let dry.

3. Using the plastic knife, spread grout all over the top of the box, making sure to get it in all the spaces between the pennies.

8. Paint the balls gold and let dry for 10 minutes. Turn the box upside down and add a squirt of glue to each corner. Put the flat side of the wood ball on the glue and press firmly. Let dry for several hours.

4. Use the damp sponge to gently wipe off the extra grout and remove any clumps around the edges. Let the box sit for 20 minutes.

5. Rinse your sponge, squeeze the water out, and then swipe it over the top of the box until the pennies show through nice and clear. Let the box sit for several hours until the grout is completely dry. Use a paper towel to remove any dust from the tops of the pennies.

9. If you want, glue on letter tiles to spell out a phrase or word.

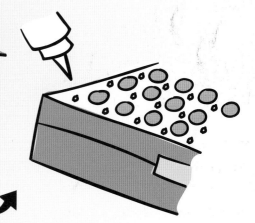

6. Add little dabs of glue to the backs of the gems and put them in between the pennies. Let dry for 30 minutes.

7. Smear craft glue around the sides of the bottom half of the box and carefully layer on the play money. Run your finger over the "bills" to smooth out any bubbles. Let dry.

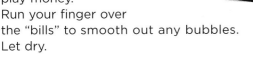

Other Ideas

✿ Use foreign coins for an international look.

✿ Mix in some silver by adding nickels, dimes, and quarters.

✿ If you don't want to use real pennies, use play coins.

Save the Earth

SLIDE MOUNT CEILING HANGING

How much do you know about protecting the Earth? It's wonderful that you don't litter and you sort your recyclable trash. But did you know that there are other ways to save the environment, while being super-crafty as well? Not all art supplies have to come from the store. When you add a recycled touch to your art designs, materials suddenly appear before you! Bottle caps, old magazines, little containers, and all kinds of odds and ends can be turned into works of wonder. Mother Earth will be so proud!

JUICY-LICIOUS POUCH PURSE

EYE-CATCHING ENVELOPES

Slide Mount Ceiling Hanging

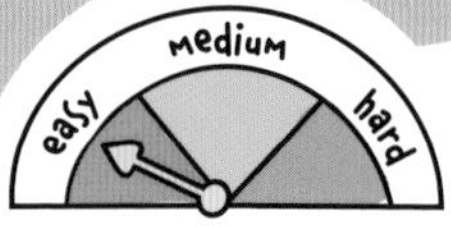

easy medium hard

Back in the day, slide mounts were what photographers used to show off their pictures. Now with the digital age, they aren't as popular (*sniffle!*) anymore. That's all right—those of us with fancy fingers can save them from the trash by using them in other ways. They happen to make perfect frames for pics from those little photo booths at the mall. To get photo mount slides, check with your local camera store to see if they have extras they're just going to throw away. You can also often find them at thrift stores.

How to Do It

1. Use the slide mount as a pattern and trace out five squares on the decorative paper. Cut out the squares and set aside.

2. Color the pictures with the highlighter pens.

STUFF YOU'LL NEED

4 or 5 slide mounts

strip of photos, cut up

highlighters in assorted colors

strand of ribbon, about 18 inches long

decorative paper

decorations, like beads, sequins, and 3-D squeeze paint

white glue

scissors

highlighter

5. Add a bit more glue on the back of each mount, over the ribbon. Get the squares you cut out in step 1. Press one square onto the back of each mount to hide the ribbon. Use your fingers to smooth out any bubbles.

3. Open a slide mount, slide a picture in, and close. Some slide mounts are already sticky inside—if not, add a tiny bit of glue around the inner flap and press it shut. Repeat for the remaining slide mounts and let dry.

4. Lay the slide mounts face down in a row. Put a little drop of glue on the back of each mount, in the center. Lay the ribbon across the mounts. This will hold them together in a line. Let dry.

6. Flip over the entire project so it's face up. Decorate each slide by gluing on beads, adding dots with 3-D squeeze paint, or whatever you want.

7. Use a thumbtack to hang the whole thing from your ceiling.

Other Ideas

* Instead of hanging the mounts from a ribbon, glue magnets on the back and stick them on your fridge or in your locker.

* Slide two photos into each slide mount so they face both ways. Sandwich the long piece of ribbon between them.

Eye-Catching Envelopes

STUFF YOU'LL NEED

assorted envelopes
leftover wrapping paper
stickers
pencil
glue stick
scissors

Plain white envelopes are so boring and bland. You need something with a little more edge. Be the domestic diva you are and make cool-looking envelopes with old wrapping paper or magazines. That way, the outside will be just as special as whatever's on the inside!

How to Do It

1. Take an envelope and carefully pull open the seams. Try not to rip it!

2. Lay the wrapping paper face down and place the open envelope on top. Lightly trace around the envelope. Cut out the shape. Set the rest of the wrapping paper aside.

3. Lay the old envelope on top of the cut-out shape and use it as a guide to fold the flaps the correct way.

4. Remove the old envelope. Apply the glue stick to the edges of the flaps to hold the new envelope together. Let dry.

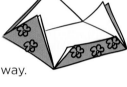

5. Flip your new, enchanting envelope over and decorate the front with stickers. If you're mailing it, glue on a solid color label for the address so the mail carrier won't have to squint to read it. After you put your letter in, use the glue stick to seal it shut.

Other Ideas

* Take some family pictures to the local copy center and make a sheet that has all the pictures on it. Use that to make your envelopes.

* You can also use old road maps, travel brochures, magazine covers, or any colorful paper that's about to be thrown out.

BE A RENEGADE RECYCLER

Turning garbage into glam is no big deal for Leah Kramer of Boston, Massachusetts. She's the founder of www.craftster.org, a web site that invites arty types of all ages to post pictures of their latest and greatest projects, many of which—you got it—make use of things we would normally throw away. Here are her tips on using recycled materials to make awesome projects.

Don't let people scare you away from creating art from tossed-out materials. Recycled crafts are hip because you're keeping something from going into a land-fill (a massive dumping ground). It takes an extra amount of creativity and thought to make something cool out of existing throwaways.

Where to get stuff

❀ Thrift stores are great sources for cloth-ing (which you can cut up for fabric or remake into new items), retro sheets and pillowcases, and cheap old records.

❀ Tobacco shops will often set aside empty cigar boxes for anyone who wants them before they get thrown away. Cigar boxes are beautiful and nicely made from wood or cardboard. These are great for crafting or for storing supplies.

❀ Wallpaper stores and stores that do interior decorating often throw out books of wallpaper and fabric samples.

❀ Print/copy shops will sometimes throw away neat "scraps" like sheets of magnets, cardboard, and odds and ends of cut paper in all kinds of colors.

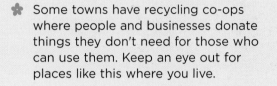

❀ Some towns have recycling co-ops where people and businesses donate things they don't need for those who can use them. Keep an eye out for places like this where you live.

❀ Thrift stores and used bookstores sell old books and magazines. Cut them up for cool images to use in your projects.

What to do with it

❀ Make cool clothes by turning old pillowcases into skirts, and by cutting up old T-shirts and then sewing them back together to make new ones.

❀ There are a million uses for the free CDs that you get in the mail. How about a disco ball made of broken CD pieces? Or a "fun house" mirror made by taking CDs and gluing them side-by-side to a board?

❀ Purses can be made from recycled things like foil juice pouches, old hard-cover books, and record album covers.

❀ Make vases or spruce up old drinking glasses by using glass etching cream to put designs onto the glass.

Remember, if we use materials that already exist, we cut back on stuff that would normally get thrown away and buried in a landfill. Reusing stuff also means we'll need fewer new things, so less will have to be manufactured. And less manufacturing means we're not using up new raw materials and not contributing to pollution. Yay!

TIPS FROM THE EXPERT

Juicy-licious Pouch Purse

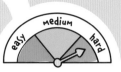

STUFF YOU'LL NEED

8 juice bags

double-stick tape

nylon trim, 1 yard long and 1 inch wide

sewing machine or extra-strong needle and thread

funky vinyl tablecloth, ½ yard (ask mom for an old one you can cut up, or buy one cheap in the dollar store)

beaded trim, 1 yard

brand-new scissors

At first glance, this bag looks like it came straight from a Beverly Hills boutique. Just wait until you see the looks on your friends' faces when you tell them it was made from foil juice bag pouches. Not only will you score points for looking super-chic, you can brag about how you saved the bags from ending up in some overflowing landfill.

How to Do It

1. Cut open the bottoms of the juice bags. Empty the juice into a pitcher and put it in the fridge. Rinse the bags out really well and prop them open on a dish drainer to dry. Smooth them with your hand to make them flat.

2. Put a piece of double-stick tape along the right-hand edge of one bag. Press another bag on the tape, connecting the two bags. Do the same with two more bags.

3. Put a long piece of tape along the bottom of one pair of bags. Take the other pair and press the top along the tape. This is one panel of your bag. Repeat with the other four bags to make a second panel.

4. Take one panel. Carefully sew it down the middle of the bags. (See page 10 for tips on sewing by hand.) When you're done, sew back and forth a tiny bit to secure the last stitch. Cut the thread.

5. Now rotate the panel. Sew along the other seam. Secure the last stitch as you did in step 4. Cut the thread. Repeat steps 4 and 5 for the other panel.

6. Put the panels on top of each other with the printed sides facing in. Sew them together, going down one side, across the bottom, and up the other side.

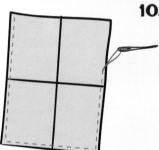

7. Get the nylon trim—this is your handle. Put a piece of double-stick tape on each end. Open the bag and press each end of the trim inside the bag at the top. Sew a square where the trim connects to the bag. Repeat for the other side.

8. Lay the vinyl face down on a table. Put pieces of double-stick tape on the top and bottom edges, sides, and center of the bag. Remove the backing from the tape. Lay the bag on the vinyl, keeping the top edges lined up. Press to stick. Fold the vinyl over to cover the back, too.

9. Fold the vinyl over the bottom of the bag (as if you were wrapping a present). Seal with more tape.

10. Put a line of tape along the top of the bag on both sides and attach beaded trim.

Other Ideas

❋ For a bigger purse, use more bags.

❋ You don't have to glue anything on the bag—you can use it with the juice bags showing.

❋ Make wallets or coin purses to go with your new purse.

❋ Cover the bag with leftover fabric instead. Or decorate it with stickers or pictures and then cover the whole thing with clear contact paper.

TIP If you are using a sewing machine, grip the bags tightly and sew at a steady pace (not too fast!). If you don't want to sew, use thin lines of E6000 glue instead.

Clip Art Treasure Chest

Ready to rock'n'roll on your
new lifestyle? Use these
precious pictures to liven
up your crafty adventures.
Make photocopies, scan them,
or trace them on fabric or
paper using carbon paper.
Or try your hand at drawing
them yourself!

Resources and Contributors

WHERE TO GET STUFF

Here's where to get the goods used in all the projects. Call or visit the web sites for more information.

🌸 **Crafter's Pick**
Makers of Crafter's Pick "The Ultimate" craft glue.
www.crafterspick.com

🌸 **Delta Technical Coatings**
Acrylic paints and general craft supplies. Sold at all major craft stores.
www.deltacrafts.com

🌸 **Diane Ribbon and Notions**
Mail-order craft supplies.
Call (602) 271-9273 or go to www.dianeribbon.com for a catalog.

🌸 **Duncan Crafts**
Makers of Tulip Fabric Glitter Spray and other general craft supplies. For questions and tips on using their products, visit www.duncancrafts.com.

🌸 **eBay**
Assorted supplies to buy on the Web. To order, visit www.ebay.com.

🌸 **Fry's Marketplace**
General grocery store for food-related items.
www.frysfood.com

🌸 **Goodwill Industries International**
National chain of thrift stores.
www.goodwill.org

🌸 **Ink It Paper Arts Store**
Assorted paper arts supplies.
www.inkitinc.com

🌸 **Jo-Ann Fabric and Crafts**
Fabric, trims, and general crafts supplies. For the store nearest you, visit www.joann.com.

🌸 **Michael's**
General craft supplies.
For the store nearest you, visit www.michaels.com.

🌸 **Stampington & Company**
Unique collection of pictures, rubber stamps, bracelet blanks, and other goodies. To order, visit www.stampington.com.

🌸 **Target**
For the store nearest you, visit www.target.com.

🌸 **Wal-Mart**
Visit www.walmart.com to find the store nearest you.

🌸 **Zia Records**
www.ziarecords.com

Acknowledgments

Chocolate ice cream with whipped cream to all the crafty divas out there who supported the first book, *The Crafty Diva's D.I.Y. Stylebook,* so much that I got invited to do another one! A lot of hard (but very fun) work went into this book—sprinkling glitter can take its toll after a while, you know! But it was so totally worth it for YOU!

A bowl of Hershey's Kisses to my husband Patrick, my son DeAngelo, and diva daughter Maya (who again helped with the ideas). Hershey Hugs to my mom and dad, Norma and David Cano; my sister Theresa; my brother David; and my sister-in-law Michelle. And chocolate sprinkles to all my friends who listened to my updates and offered me quad mochas to keep me on track: Tracy Dove Coppen, Laurie Notaro, Jean Railla, Jenny Hart, Nancy Marmolejo, Michelle Savoy, Maria Fowler, Ashley Farmer, Shannon Johnson, Vanessa Brady, Randy Cordova, Richard Ruelas, Daniel Gonzalez, Anita Mabante Leach, Terri Ouellette, as well as my mom-in-law Susie Murillo for helping me with sixteen loads of laundry at deadline time!

I couldn't have made these chapters exciting without the help of my crafty home girls. A hunk of double-fudge chocolate cake to Sadie Jo Smokey (Skinny Scarf); Lara Piu (Oh Oh Oatmeal Facial Mask and Peppermint Pick-Me-Up Face Mist); Jaimee Rose (Girl Power Message Soaps and Horoscope Bath Salts); Keri Plezia (Power Pop-up Cards, Nifty Note Holders, and Happy Hangers); the lovely ladies who contributed their time for the sidebars and features; my artsy *amigas* at GetCrafty.com, Supernaturale.com, and Craftster.org; the crew at Diane Ribbon and

Notions (Arizona's oldest crafts warehouse, 55 years strong!); Marguerite at the Purple Lizard; and the staff at Michael's and Jo-Ann's, who were always nice and helpful no matter how many times I asked for the very things they were out of. As always, a double shot of espresso to Jineane Ford and Amy Brooke at KPNX, Channel 12, the gang at *Good Morning Arizona,* and to Kerry Lengel, Nicole Carroll, Tami Thornton, and Randy Lovely of *The Arizona Republic,* for always supporting my crafty endeavors outside of the newsroom. A tall malted milkshake to my agents at WMA: Scott Wachs and Jonathan Pecarsky.

Most of all, a big thank-you-with-sugar-on-top to Carrie Wheeler for her wonderful illustrations, John Samora for the perfect photography, Margo Mooney for the magical layout, and, saving the best for last, Julie Mazur and the Watson-Guptill team for making this all come together.

143

Index